SECRETS OF THE KUJI

By MIYAI YASUTAI
Published 1787

Ku	Ji	Hi	Den
九	字	秘	傳
Nine	Kanji	Secret	Teaching

Translator: Eric Shahan
Transcription: Iida Kazuhiro

Copyright © 2024 Eric Michael Shahan
All Rights Reserved.
ISBN: 978-1-950959-74-7

SECRETS OF THE KUJI・九字秘傳

Translator's Introduction

This is a reprint and translation of *Secrets of the Kuji*, an illustrated guide to using the Kuji, the Nine Seals. It includes many methods for making as well as how to make talisman. It was published in 1787 by a mathematician named Miyai Yasutai (also read as Miyai Yasuhiro)宮井安泰 (1760~1815.)

Miyai was a member of the Kanazawa clan in Kaga Domain, which is now part of Ishikawa Prefecture. Recent research indicates that Miyai also trained in Ninjutsu.

According to researcher Kasahara Shinji 笠原愼治

Miyai's great-uncle was a man named Murai Tonomono, the second generation head of the Kanazawa clan. He was accused of a crime and was ordered to commit seppuku. Murai's nephew, Miyai Jubei was banished. Jubei travelled to Iga Domain and trained ninjutsu along with his son Miyai Yasutai, before they were allowed to return to what is modern day Ichikawa prefecture.

Thus Miyai Yasutai is thought to have studied a Kaga-Iga Ryu Ninpo 加賀伊賀流忍法 *a type of Ninjutsu that was a combination of his studies in Iga combined with martial arts of Kaga...Kaga Domain had sixty Ninja in its employ.*

-Secrets of Miyai Yasutai, Mathmatics Instructor at Kaga Domain Meirindo Academy
藩校明倫堂算学師範宮井安泰の秘密
2013

Miyai also published many books on surveying techniques and mathematics. He died on August 22nd 1815 at the age of 56.

Terminology:

Kuji – The Nine Chinese Characters. Also known as the Nine Seals.
Kanji – Chinese Characters. Japan did not have a written language before encountering the Chinese. Originally documents were all written in Chinese, however over the centuries a Japanese way of using the Kanji developed.
Mudra – Hand Gestures

ERIC SHAHAN · MIYAI YASUTAI

SECRETS OF THE KUJI・九字秘傳

ERIC SHAHAN · MIYAI YASUTAI

Kuji Hiden
九字秘傳
Secrets of the Kuji
(cover)

九字秘傳

金澤 宮井安泰 著

總論

夫九字ノ傳授ハ兵ノ一法トシテ、更ニ卯明ヲ加ヘテ護身法ト同ク佛家ヨリ傳之ヲ共ニ兵法ノ奥儀トシテ大ヒニコレヲ尊ブ。而モ不分明ノ説ヲ附會シ、其傳既ニ真ヲ失フ。然ニ各其起元アリ。佛家ニ於テ九字ノ義ハ其本ヲノ事ハ佛家ニ精シ、九字ノ義ハ其本ヲ不傳、古来道家ノ傳トメ其起元ヲ精ス。九字傳ト四縱五橫傳各異ナリ。抱朴子

Secrets of Kuji
By Miyai Yasutai of Kanazawa
Published 1787

Soron 総論
General Introduction

Generally speaking, Kuji is a method taught as part of military strategy and is contained in many swordfighting schools. It is a combination of *Inmyo* 印明, hand gestures accompanied by sacred words, with a *Goshin Ho* 護身法 self-protection method, that derives from Buddhist teachings. Schools of martial arts will often record the secrets of Kuji in their documents of transmission. However, these lessons are only taught to the highest level students since they are considered to be *Okugi* 奥義 inner mysteries of sword schools. A person that has become enlightened to Kuji treasures that understanding.

While many details regarding the origin of Kuji are unclear or have been lost to time, the *Inmyo* 印明, hand gestures accompanied by sacred words, as well as the *Goshin Ho* 護身法 self-protection method, each originated separately and were later combined into one method.

Goshin Ho 護身法
Self-Protection Method

Buddhism discusses Self-Protection Methods extensively, however Buddhist texts do not discuss the meaning of each of the nine Kanji that make up the Kuji.

For the meanings of the Kanji you have to look to Taoist sources. Books related to Taoism contain detailed descriptions of the origins of the Kanji that make Taoism in ancient times.

内篇ニ曰、山ニ入ルトキハ、宜ク六甲秘祝ヲ知ルベシ。祝ニ曰、臨兵闘者皆陳列前行。凡九字常ニ當ニ密ニ之ヲ祝スベシト。今用ル所ノ九字ハ左字ニ行アリ。又九字ニ卯契ヲ附會シタル字ナリシ。又九字ニハ亦此義慮説也。弘法大師ナリト傳レリ。トモ云ヘリ。予其義ヲ不レ知ト雖モ世ノ人ノ用ル書、抱朴子欅下虜草或ハ軍林寶鑑等ニ出ル所ヲ真トメ、大畧正レ之為一篇、其類ナルヲ以テ佛家ノ傳ヲ併セ寶鑑等ニ出ル所ヲ以テ、佛家ノ傳ヲ併セ記シ、次ニ兵家者流ニ秘傳ト稱スルモノヲ書ス。且附會ニ似タリト雖モ署其

The Four Vertical and Five Horizontal Lines

The *Yon Tate, Go Yoko Den* 四縦五横伝 the Four Vertical and Five Horizontal Lines and the Kuji originated from different sources.

The *Inner Chapter* of the book *Baopuzi* 抱朴子 or *The Master Who Embraces Simplicity*[1] advises,

When travelling through the mountains, you should protect yourself by chanting the Rokko Hishu, *Secret Sixty Year*[2] *spell.*

---

[1] The *Baopuzi* 抱朴子 or *The Master Who Embraces Simplicity* is known in Japanese as *Hobokushi*. It was written in 317 AD by the Taoist practitioner, philosopher, physician and politician Ge Hong (283~343 AD.) It is divided into twenty *Inner Chapters* and Fifty-two *Outer Chapters*. The inner chapters deal with Senjutsu, or Taoist Immortal Techniques, such as longevity and immortality. The *Outer Chapters* is a Confucian political treatise that discusses the merits and demerits of politics, as well as good and evil in human affairs. Thus the book is commonly known as *The Inner and Outer Books of Taoism.*

[2] *Rokko Hishu* 六甲秘祝, *In Praise of the Secret Sixty Cycles*. This refers to the sixty-year Sexagenary cycle, which is a sixty-term cycle of Twelve Earthly Branches, represented by the twelve animals of the zodiac, combined with Ten Heavenly Stems. The author uses the Kanji 祝 which is a word that typically means "celebration" but in combination with 秘 "secret" it means "to transfer calamity to another place."

To use this spell chant the following incantation,

Rin, Pyo, Toh, Sha , Kai, Jin, Retsu, Zen, Gyo
臨　兵　闘　者　皆　陣　列　前　行

As individual words this incantation means,

Face, Soldier, Fight, Person, Everything, Legion, Arrange, Before, Conduct

As a sentence this means:

Celestial soldiers, descend and conduct yourselves before me!

The Master Who Embraces Simplicity cautions that the secret of the Kuji should not be revealed to others and always be chanted in secrecy. The Kuji used these days replaces the Kanji *Gyo* 行 Conduct with the Kanji *Zai* 在 Exist. [3]

The Kuji which includes the Kanji *Zai* 在 Exist, but without *Gyo* 行 Conduct is as follows,

Rin, Pyo, Toh, Sha , Kai, Jin, Retsu, Zai, Zen
臨　兵　闘　者　皆　陣　列　在　前
Face, Soldier, Fight, Person, Everything,
Legion, Arrange, Exist, Before
Celestial soldiers, descend and arrange yourselves before me!

It is also said that the famous Buddhist priest Kobo Daishi[4] was the one who paired the symbolic hand gestures and nine Kanji, however there are some who say this is not a true story. As for myself, I do not know the whether this legend is true or not.

---

[3] The English translation of each Kanji in the Kuji is approximate as the meaning of each Kanji can change according to the incantation being employed or by the school.

[4] "The Grand Master who Propagated the Dharma." Also known as Kukai 空海 (774 ~835.)

There are some books like *The Master Who Embraces Simplicity: Underneath the Sakura Trees, the Grass Rots* [5] as well as *The Treasure Grove of Military Knowledge* [6] which contain information that I have found to be generally true, so I have included sections of those books in this work.

Thus, this book will contain information from similar books as well as information regarding the transmission of Kuji methods from Buddhism and secret traditions found in sword fighting schools. I will expand on these texts with additional information.

---

[5] 櫻下腐草 *Underneath the Sakura trees, the grass rots.* This seems to relate to the classic saying *Kusaretaru Kusa Hotaru To naru* 腐草為蛍 which means "the grass withers and rots to become fireflies." Up to the late Edo Era, before science had advanced, the people believed that fireflies were spontaneously created in areas of overgrown grass that covered the rotting roots of bamboo plants. It is not clear what this phrase has to do with *The Master Who Embraces Simplicity*, possibly *Underneath the Sakura trees, the grass rots* is an alternate name.

[6] *Gunrin Hokan* 軍林寶鑑 *The Treasure Grove of Military Knowledge.* Written by Shi Shibi 施子美 during the Muromachi Period (1336~1573.)

可ナルヲ選ブ。亦聽音ヲ以テ補フ之者也

九字太公望傳

太公使周公旦ヲ為相。先ヅ令ス齋スル七日。而後授與ス此之大要。凧對嚴出之山卯。當テ左掌握リ心。一端伸テ右掌五指ヲ向外。一度招下之ノ咒ヲ曰。臣人相對并三口。臣人一品字ニ相合メ作ニス臨ノ字ヲ。
心ノ一端伸左ノ掌五指ヲ向外一度招下之ノ咒ヲ曰。兵ノ一字ヲ爲シ十六兩下漆ニ八ニ降リ十六ノ兩ヲ相合メ作ニ兵ノ一字ヲ
兩掌向外ニ置ヲ在乳邊咒ヲ曰。門ノ裡ニ栽ヱ豆長シ。一
寸。合門ヲ作ル寸相寫。兩掌横椎ニ兩乳端咒ヲ曰。二十
日中下十斜。者ハ十一ノ日一ノ十ノ下一ノ十八斜ノ相合メ作ル拳兩掌ヲ押ニ兩ノ
乳端咒ヲ曰。兩相并金鳥飛ヒ。金鳥ハ日則日ノ相合メ

九字太公望伝
Kuji as Transmitted by Duke Tai of Qi[7]

When the military commander Duke Tai of Qi was in the service of the Zhou Dynasty, he made the Duke of Zhou[8] purify himself for a period of seven days.[9] Afterwards, Duke Tai gave the Duke of Zhou a book on the fundamentals of Kuji. It describes both how the Kuji should be done as well as the underlying meaning of each of the nine Kanji,

Early in the morning, face the east where you can see the first rays of sunrise. [10] *If you are in the mountains face the ridgeline to the east, if you are in flatlands, face the horizon. Place the palm of your left hand on your chest and grip, while extending the five fingers of your right hand in front of you with your palm down.*

---

[7] Duke Tai of Qi 太公望 (1128~1015 BC.) Also known as Jiang Ziya.
[8] Duke of Zhou 周公旦 (?~?, reigned 1042~1035 BC.)
[9] *Mono Imi* 物忌 Purifying the body and mind through seclusion, fasting and abstinence before an important ceremony. In Onmyodo practice, this consists of home confinement on inauspicious days to avoid misfortune.
[10] *Madaki ni Ton Shutsu no San-u* 夙に暾出之山卯. Early in the morning look to where the sun shines on the side of a mountain.

Turn your hands palms down curl your fingers once toward you as if you are beckoning someone. Chant the incantation,[11]

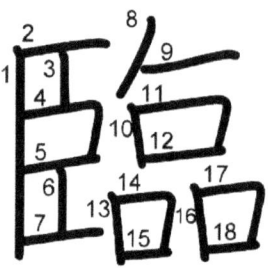

Rin 臨 (to) Face
The retainers are lined up like the Kanji mouth repeated three times.

The Kanji for retainer is *Shinjin* 臣人 and the Kanji for mouth is *Kuchi* 口, thus joining the two-Kanji combination for retainer 臣 with three mouths, 口, 口, 口, creates the Kanji *Rin* 臨 meaning "to face."[12]

---

[11] The Kanji *Ju* 呪 can refer to either a curse, a spell or an incantation. It means to borrow the power of a deity or mystical object to remove misfortune or illness, or to bring misfortune upon others. While you are not drawing the Kanji for this incantation, understanding how they are written is important to understanding the Kuji so the stroke order is included.

[12] The second Kanji of retainer, 人 is altered to fit above the three mouths 品. Traditionally this Kanji is a person lying down (臥→臤 is how the Kanji adapts to fit the other element) and observing the state of 品 something.

Next, place your right palm above your heart and extend the fingers of your left hand out in front of you before lowering your hand. Chant the incantation,

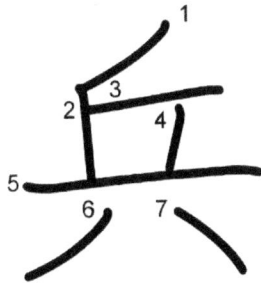

Hei 兵 Soldier
Underneath sixteen coins, place the numbers one and an eight.

This is a reference to the era of King Jie, of the Xia dynasty (1728~1675 BC.) In that era, the government fixed the price they paid for a loaf of bread that was given to a soldiers as a ration at sixteen coins. In both Chinese and Japanese, loaves of bread are counted with the Kanji *Kin* 斤 meaning "one loaf (of bread.)" Thus "underneath sixteen coins," means "underneath the Kanji for a soldier's ration of bread" write the Kanji for one 一 and the Kanji for eight 八.[13]

Therefore to create the Kanji *Hyo* 兵 or "soldier" write the Kanji for *a loaf of bread* 斤 with Kanji for the numbers *one* 一 and *eight* 八 underneath. [14]

---

[13] King Jie (Chinese: 桀; traditionally 1728~1675 BC) was the 17th and last ruler of the Xia dynasty of China. He is traditionally regarded as a tyrant and oppressor who brought about the collapse of a dynasty

[14] The original character is a combination of 斤 which means "axe," and 廾 which means "two-handed" So a man with an axe in both hands.

Next, turn the palms of your hands outward and hold them at the level of your chest. Chant the incantation,

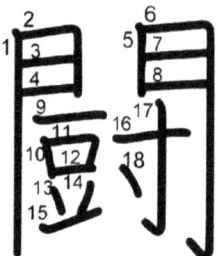

Toh 闘 Fight
Plant a bean behind the gate and it will sprout one out of the earth.

To create the Kanji *Toh* 闘 "fight," means you start with the Kanji *Mon* 門 meaning "gate." Then you add the Kanji *Mame* 豆 meaning "bean" and *Sun* 寸 referring to an old Japanese unit of measure equivalent to 3 centimeters/1 inch.

Next, move the palms of your hands out to the left and right so they are on either side of your chest. Chant the incantation,

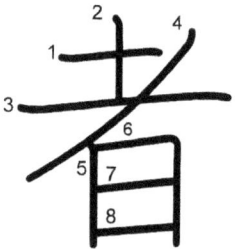

Sha 者 Person
When you write the twentieth, you are writing "two tens" and day.

In Japanese, the twentieth day of any month is pronounced *Hatsuka* and is written with the number two 二 the number ten 十 and the word day 日 resulting in the word "twentieth." Thus you can also write "the twentieth" with: ten 十 ten 十 day 日. If you then take the vertical stroke 丨 of the second ten 十 and turn it sideways 丿 you get "the day of ten, ten" 十十丿日 By then combining ten 十 ten 十 of 丿 day 日 you get the Kanji *Sha* 者 meaning person.

Squeeze both palms in fists, press them both to your breast. Chant the incantation,

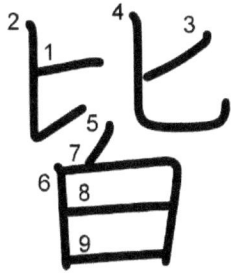

Kai 皆 Everything
Standing two abreast, the gold crows fly off

A gold crow[15] refers to the sun, so can be represented by the Kanji 日, which means sun. Next, double the element ヒ and place them ヒヒ above the Kanji 日 to arrive at the Kanji *Kai* 皆 everything.[16]

---

[15] Kinu 金烏 Gold crow refers to the three-legged crow that is said to inhabit the sun. Thus Kinu refers to the sun. Similarly Gyokuto 玉兎 jeweled rabbit, refers to the rabbit that is said to inhabit the moon.

[16] The text does not mention what the element ヒ represents. In Japanese the element ヒ can refer to spoon or a knife without a hand guard. Traditionally, this Kanji is explained as combining the Kanji Shiroi 白 white, which in its basic means "to say" with the Kanji Hi 比 "people are lined up." Thus "people saying the same thing" or "all." say the same thing, which in turn means "all."

作皆之字伸兩掌向身掛兩肩呪曰小猿獨立
只牽車猿猶邑小邑古文作阝阝車相合作陣字兩掌向身押
勝間呪曰殘字脫右利脫左殘字脫右則歹利脫左則
刀刀刂也歹刂相合例列之字兩掌伸押兩膝呪曰劈一
力人前抱土一人土相合作在字擧兩掌成斗衝呪
曰九月中旬磨一刀八一算合成九刀則刂也八一月刂相合
作前之字此上九者穀干天陰干地天地者君臣也鑷
能此九者則合三光日大陽月大陰星辰謂之三光達九
曜日月木火土金水謂之七曜羅睺計者連前七曜謂九曜轉二十八
宿轉移也宿音秀星也東方角亢氐房心尾箕北方斗牛女虛危室壁西方奎婁胃昴畢觜參南方井鬼柳星張翼軫謂之二十八宿安四時春爲青陽夏爲朱明秋爲白藏冬爲玄英謂之四時穩四天蒼天昊天旻天上天謂之四天

Extend the fingers of both hand and turn them towards yourself, placing them on your shoulders. Chant the incantation,

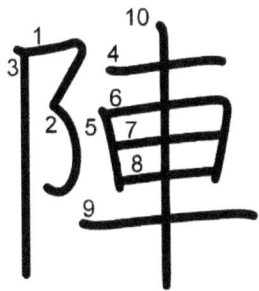

Jin 陣 Legion
There is a small monkey there alone pulling a cart. The monkey seems like he is part of a village.

There is a small monkey pulling a cart車 alone. The monkey seems like he is part of a village邑.

A small village邑 can be abbreviated as ß and is placed on the left. By starting with an element that stands for small village ß on the left and cart 車 to the right, creates the Kanji Jin陣 meaning military encampment.[17]

---

[17] The Kanji 邑, which means small village, can be abbreviated as the element ß as if the entire Kanji has been compressed. It is then used to form other Kanji. The element ß on its own can be read as Ozato, which means "a large village." However, it can also be read as Ozaru, which also means "a large village" but contains the word Zaru, which can also mean "monkey."

Since the Kanji 陣 is referring to a small village, the element ß is Kozato, small village, or Kozaru, small monkey.

This same concept appears in a *Yamato Ryu Kyudo Densho* 大和流弓道伝書 Yamato School Archery document,

A solitary tiny monkey stands alone and only pulls cart. I have been told that this Kanji represents a monkey and a small village. The ancient people said that when you have a small village the Kanji 邑 is reduced to ß. By joining the Kanji for cart 車 to ß you end up with the Kanji 陣.

Turn your palms so they are facing you and press them into your hips. Chant the incantation,

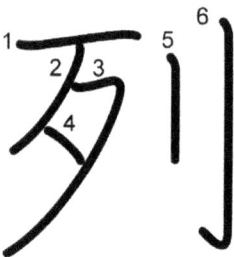

Retsu 列 Line
Remove the element meaning to damage from the right side of the Kanji to remain.

The Kanji *Zan* 残 means "remain." Remove the element 戔 from the right side of the Kanji. This element means "to damage." There is also the Kanji *Ri* 利 which means "to benefit." Remove the 禾 element from the left side. This element means "grains."

Having removed 禾 "grains" from the left side of benefit 利 and removed 戔 "to damage" from the right side of remain 残, all that is left are the elements 歹, which means "the bare bones of a skeleton" and 刂 which is an abbreviation of the Kanji *Katana* 刀 meaning sword.

By joining "bare bones" 歹 with "sword" 刂 we get the Kanji *Retsu* 列 to arrange in a line.

Extend both palms and press them into your knees. Chant the incantation,

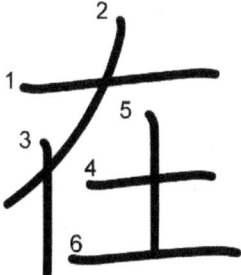

Zai 在 Exist
The first person who holds power and authority holds the earth in front of him.

This is why the Kanji *Zai* 在 existence, is a combination of the Kanji *Hitori* 一人 one person and the Kanji *Tsuchi* 土 soil.

Raise both palms to form *Dozu* 斗衝, the north star. Chant the incantation,

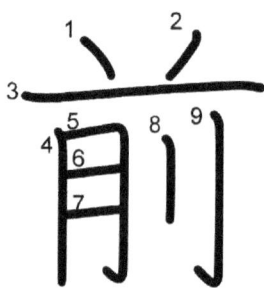

Zen 前 Face
In the middle of the ninth month,[18] *polish one Katana.*

Add together the Kanji *Ichi* 一 one and *Hachi* 八 eight gives you the Kanji *Kyu* 九 Nine. The Kanji *Katana* 刀 can also be abbreviated to the element 刂 which stands for sword. Thus combining *Hachi* 八 Eight, *Ichi* 一 One, *Tsuki* 月 Moon and 刂 the element referring to a sword we arrive at the Kanji *Zen* 前 to Face.[19]

---

[18] Under the old calendar system the ninth month equates to October. In autumn, the cold of a river cuts into the skin. Thus the a sword a sharp sword can be said to cut like cold fall water cuts the skin. The Kanji 前 can be broken down as follows. The top section can be split into the number one 一 and the number eight 八, in turn these numbers can be added together to form the number nine. The element on the bottom left of the Kanji is 月 which means both moon and month. Thus combining nine and month gives us the ninth month. The final element of the Kanji is "sword" 刂 which gives us "a sword sharpened in the ninth month so it cuts cleanly like cold autumn water."

[19] For a recreation of this sequence, see the photos starting on page 225.

These nine Kanji also contain the secret of the vast and distant Heaven while concealing the vast and distant Earth. The relationship between heaven and earth can be thought of as being the same as the relationship between the ruler and the ruled. Between the master and the servant. These nine Kanji are also referred to as *Sanko ni Hikanai* 三光に合 the Unification of the Three Brightnesses. The Three Lights are *Nichi-getsu-Seishin* 日月星辰 Day, Moon and Celestial Bodies.

Day 日 represents the Sun 太陽, the greatest possible manifestation of *Yo*, or Yang. Moon represents the moon, the greatest possible manifestation of *In* 大陰, or Yin. Celestial Bodies 星辰 refers to all the stars and planets as well as celestial phenomenon like comets.

There is another word for the Three Brightnesses. That is *Kuyo* 九曜 the Nine Brightnesses, which refers to the nine visible celestial bodies that can affect the Earth. The Nine Brightnesses can be further divided into two parts. The first is *Shichiyo* 七曜 the Seven Luminaries.

The Seven Luminaries are the seven celestial bodies visible from earth. From the brightest to dimmest: the Sun, the Moon, Venus, Jupiter, Mars, Mercury and Saturn.

The second part of the Nine Brightnesses consists of solar and lunar eclipses. By adding *Rahu* 羅睺, solar eclipses, and *Ketu* 計都, lunar eclipses to the seven luminaries, we get the *Kuyo* 九曜 the Nine Brightnesses.

Next, I would like to discuss *Nijuhasshu* 二十八宿 the Twenty-Eight Mansions.

The Twenty-Eight Mansion imagines the sky as a circle divided into four sections, which are each further divided into seven sub-divisions, for a total of twenty-eight. Each division and sub-division are contain a representative animal or object. The Twenty-Eight Mansions rotate and by rotate, I mean that they are in motion. The word Mansions is indicated by the Kanji 宿 which is normally read as Shuku, however here it is read as Shu and refers to the constellations.

The Eastern Section Includes the Following Constellations
1. 角 Horn
2. 亢 Neck
3. 氐 Root
4. 房 Room
5. 心 Heart
6. 尾 Tail
7. 箕 Winnowing Basket

The Northern Section Includes the Following Constellations
8. 斗 Southern Dipper
9. 牛 Ox
10. 女 Girl
11. 虛 Emptiness
12. 危 Rooftop
13. 室 Encampment
14. 壁 Wall

The Western Section Includes the Following Constellations
15. 奎 Legs
16. 婁 Bond
17. 胃 Stomach
18. 昴 Hairy Head
19. 畢 Net
20. 觜 Turtle Beak
21. 參 Three Stars

The Northern Section Includes the Following Constellations
22. 井 Well
23. 鬼 Ghost
24. 柳 Willow
25. 星 Star
26. 張 Extended
27. 翼 Wings
28. 軫 Chariot

These are collectively known as the Twenty-Eight Mansions or Twenty-Eight Constellations.

Shiji 四時 The Four Seasons

A simple explanation of *Shiji* 四時, the four seasons, each of which has a corresponding color.

The word spring is indicated by the color *Seiyo* 青陽, the emerging green of early spring.

The word summer is indicated by the color *Shuka* 朱明 a type of vermillion that describes a period of swelling, flowering, expanding with heat based on the Five Agents Fire, Water, Wood, Metal, and Earth.

The word fall is indicated by the color *Hakuzo* 日藏 pure white reflecting how the autumn harvest fills up the storehouse.

The word winter is indicated by the color *Genei* 元英 black, the color of winter.

These are known as the *Shiji*, four times or the four seasons.

Shiten 四天 The four types of pleasant sky.

1. *Soden* 蒼天 blue heaven, describing the clear skies of spring
2. *Koten* 昊天 summer sky, describing the bright light pouring down in summer.
3. *Binten* 旻天 the autumn sky.
4. *Joten* 上天 the sky in winter.

These are the types of sky found in each season.

豊八節ニ立春春分立夏夏至立秋秋無災五
方東方北東方東南方ハ水ニ属木中ニ属央火ハ金土ニ属ニ属南方ハ無名四
維之属者自子至乾ニ謂西北之ヲ巽謂之ニ東属南謂之坤謂之四
之人十ニ定ノ十支西ニ属属乾トニ属祥農ヲ轉ジ凶ヲ不溺ル不顕ニ地利ニ吉十二時夜半ヨリ癸
和四民工商農五畜睦ニ公男侯ニ伯也故上不違天象天變
時下不廣地利中ニ獲人和何懼之有哉
張商英注曰儲選芥鉞之威擒敵之
邑ノ權ヲ闘治國安家以快民意者得三才
之不欠以安將意皆天意入テ天子心風調
雨順穀足國冨百民ヲ不知饑寒之患陣廟
神乾ノ軍門去災袄却疾病ニ列増軍健兵以

Hassetsu 八節
The eight periods marking the beginning and end of each season

1. *Risshun* 立春 The first day of spring which is approximately February 4.
2. *Shunbun* 春分 vernal equinox, March 20~21st.
3. *Rikka* 立夏 first day of summer around May 6th
4. *Geshi* 夏至 summer solstice, the longest day of the year.
5. *Risshun* 立秋 first day of autumn around August 8th
6. *Shunbun* 秋分 Autumnal Equinox around September 22~24th
7. *Ritto* 立冬 First day of winter around November 8th
8. *Toji* 冬至 winter solstice, the shortest day of the year.

Goho ni Wazawai ga Nai 五方災いが無い
Kuji will prevent calamities in all Five Directions and across all Five Agents[20]

The five directions are East, associated with wood, West which is associated with metal, South which is associated with fire, North, which is associated with water and center which is associated with earth. These are known as the Five Directions.

Shi-I 四維
Preventing Disasters in the four ordinal directions with Kuji

1. *Tatsumi* 巽 is associated with southeast.
2. *Hitsuji Saru* 坤 is associated with southwest
3. *Ushitora* 艮 is associated with northeast.
4. *Inui* 乾 is associated with northwest.

---

[20] The Five Agents in order are:
Wood 木 → Fire 火 → Earth 土 → Metal 金 → Water 水

Kanshi 幹支 There is luck in the Main Branches

Kanshi 幹支 are the ten Stems and Twelve Branches that form the sixty year sexagenary cycle. The system can also be called *Eto* 干支. The Twelve Earthly Branches are represented by the twelve animals of the zodiac, combined with Ten Heavenly Stems, thus it is known as the Stems and Branches. The Stems repeat six times, each time pairing with a different branch.

The branches are comprised of the twelve animals: Rat, Ox, Tiger, Rabbit, Dragon, Snake, Horse, Goat, Monkey, Rooster, Dog, Pig. The cycle begins with Turtle Shell paired with Rat and Ends with Grass for Liberation is paired with Pig. A person can become unlucky in this cycle but then lucky again.

	Ten Heavenly Stems 幹		Twelve Earthly Branches 支
1	*Ko* 甲 turtle shell	1	*Ne* 子 Rat
2	*Otsu* 乙 fish guts	2	*Ushi* 丑 Ox
3	*Hei* 丙 fishtail	3	*Tora* 寅 Tiger
4	*Tei* 丁 nail	4	*U* 卯 Rabbit
5	*Bo* 戊 halberd	5	*Tatsu* 辰 Dragon
6	*Ki* 己 threads on a loom	6	*Mi* 巳 Snake
7	*Kanoe* 庚 evening star	7	*Uma* 午 Horse
8	*Shin* 辛 to offend superiors	8	*Hitsuji* 未 Sheep
9	*Jin* 壬 burden	9	*Saru* 申 Monkey
10	*Ki* 癸 grass for libation	10	*Tori* 酉 Rooster
		11	*Inu* 戌 Dog
		12	*I* 亥 Pig

Juniji ni Yoshi de Aru 十二時に吉である
Using Kuji can bring you luck any hour of the day.

Niju-ji, refers to the twelve, two-hour intervals that make up a day. While generally speaking they are referred to by the twelve animals of the zodiac, there are other names. In addition, saying *From Midnight to Doors are Locked and Everyone is Asleep* can refer to a full day.

Yahan 夜半 Midnight	*Ne* 子 Rat	11 pm ~1am
Keimei 鶏鳴 Rooster Call	*Ushi* 丑 Ox	1~3am
Heitan 平旦 Daybreak	*Tora* 寅 Tiger	3~5 am
Nisshutsu 日出 Dawn	*U* 卯 Rabbit	5~7 am
Shokuji 食時 Mealtime	*Tatsu* 辰 Dragon	7~9 am
Guchu 隅中 Midday	*Mi* 巳 Snake	9~11 am
Nicchu 日中 Noon	*Uma* 午 Horse	11am~1pm
Nittetsu 日昳 Afternoon	*Hitsuji* 未 Sheep	1~3 pm
Hoji 哺時 Evening	*Saru* 申 Monkey	3~5 pm
Nichinyu 日入 Sunset	*Tori* 酉 Rooster	5~7 pm
Kokon 黄昏 Twilight	*Inu* 戌 Dog	7~9 pm
Ninjyo 人定 Doors locked & everyone is asleep	*I* 亥 Pig	9~11 pm

鬼柳星張翼軫
謂之二十八宿ト也
冬ヲ謂フ元英ト
謂之四時
春分立夏夏至
立秋秋ヲ謂之八節
分立冬冬至立春ヲ謂之八節
南方屬火比方屬水
中央屬土謂之五方
屬艮西北八維
乾ヲ謂之四維
者轉凶
為祥也
氣天河星斗風雲雨雪煙霞霧露雪雹虹蜺
天閃電雷霆霹靂霜霰折雪煙靄雹永凌日暈
月珥薄蝕霰霓滋潤旱魃潦池霖
露連縣朦朧朧魑芋ノ属謂之乾氣ト

吉十二時刻謂之十二時
自半夜至人定
自子至亥謂之十二支
祥幹支自甲至癸謂之十千幹自

穩四天蒼夫昊天旻夫謂之四天
安四時春為青暘夏為
朱明秋為白藏
無咎四維南属坤東南屬巽
東方属
無災五方西方屬金
豊八節春

不溺于乾
不蹶坤利

Do not become obsessed with *Kenki* 乾氣 the various meteorological phenomena. In other words do not allow the weather to overcome your reasoning.[21]

Tenga 天河	The milky way
Seito 星斗	Celestial bodies
Fu-un 風雲	Clouds blown across the sky
Usetsu 雨雪	Rain and snow
Enka 煙霞	Smoke and mist
Muro 霧露	Fog and Mist
Seppaku 雪雹	Snow and Large Hail
Kogei 虹蜺	Rainbow
Senden 閃電	Lightning
Raitei 雷霆	Severe Thunder
Hekireki 霹靂	Thunder and Lightning
Sosan 霜霰	Frost and Small Hail
Sakusetsu 霖雪	Snow related
Enai 煙靄	Mist
Hyoryo 氷凌	Ice
Higasa 日暈	Red halo around sun
Getsuji 月珥	Ring of light around the moon
Hakushoku 薄蝕	The sun or moon appearing hazy
Aitai 靉靆	Clouds or mist hanging low
Jijun 滋潤	Rain making everything slippery
Kanbatsu 旱魃	Insufficient rain
Boda 滂沱	Heavy Rain
Rinin 霖霪	Long rainy period
Renmen 連緜	Unknown, possibly rainy skies
Moro 朦朧	Darkness from mist
Soryu 颼飅	Light breeze

---

[21] The *Kenki* are not described in this book. The list is from the 14th c. book *The Treasure Grove of Military Knowledge.* By Shi Shibi.

Tensho 天象 **Heavenly Conditions**
Tenpen 天変 **Heavenly Changes**

Tensho, heavenly conditions, revers to changes in the weather. *Tenpen*, heavenly changes, refer to unusual conditions in the sky like violent winds, lightning, eclipses or weather that results in natural disasters.

Konri ni Tsuzukazu 坤利に躑かず
Do not hesitate due to the terrain. [22]

The principle of *Chi no Ri* 地利, means to take full advantage of the terrain. This includes not hesitating when faced with rugged terrain.

---

[22] The fifty-six types of terrain are not described in this book. The list on the following four pages is from the 14th century book *The Treasure Grove of Military Knowledge*. By Shi Shibi. As the terms are not defined, some of them are unknown or unclear.

SECRETS OF THE KUJI・九字秘傳

鬼柳星張翼軫 直忍反

謂之二十八宿也

謂之元英 冬

謂之四時

春分立夏夏至立秋秋

分立冬冬至謂之八節

中央屬土謂之五方

南方屬火北方屬水

屬艮西北屬

乾謂之四維

者轉凶為祥也

氣閃電雷霆霹靂霜雹霰霖雪煙霧靄雲霓虹蜺

月珥薄蝕霰霓滋潤旱魃滂沱霖氷凌日暈

露連緜朦朧曨𩃿芋屬之乾氣

安四時

豊八節

無咎四維

無災五方

東方屬木春

南方屬坤東北

西方屬金

東南屬巽

夫蒼天昊天旻天四天

春爲青陽夏爲朱明秋爲白藏

自甲至癸謂之十干自子至亥謂之十二支祥

吉十二時 自半夜至人定謂之十二時 不溺于乾氣不蹶坤利

1.	*Gogaku* 五嶽	The five sacred mountains in China
2.	*Shitoku* 四瀆	The four great rivers of China
3.	*Kyutaku* 九澤	Connected marshlands
4.	*Hassui* 八水	Eight sources of water (? Unknown)
5.	Goko 五湖	The five great lakes of ancient China
6.	Kyuko 九江	Nine rivers of (modern day) Jiujiang City
7.	Sankyo 三峽	The Three Gorges
8.	Kaitai 海岱	An alternate name for Mt. Tai 泰山
9.	Sentaku 川澤	Where rivers and marshlands meet
10.	Sansui 山水	Mountain rivers
11.	Keikan 溪澗	Ravine
12.	Hato 陂塘	Dyke
13.	Haro 波浪	The swell of ocean waves
14.	Niwatazumi 潦流	Puddles that collect after rain
15.	Choto 潮濤	Waves at high tide
16.	Koko 港泒	Seaport (?)
17.	*Hikibaitan* 匹賣反	Describing the land around the shore (?)
18.	Satan 沙灘	Gravely beach
19.	Haran 波瀾	Large and small waves
20.	Teishu 汀洲	Shallow river with a sandy bottom
21.	Koro 潢潦	Water collecting on the road
22.	Bakufu 瀑布	A cloth rippling in the wind, a waterfall.
23.	Shimagi 島岐	Islands that emerge at low tide (?)
24.	Kozan 溝壐	Drainage ditch
25.	Kyori 橋梁	Bridge
26.	Kodo 河度	Crossing a river during a battle
27.	Kanshin 關津	Government crossing checkpoint
28.	Gaisai 涯漈	A cliff with breaking waves at the bottom
29.	Hoshuku 浦淑	Clear water by the shore
30.	Tomon 斗門	Flood gate

五嶽 四瀆 九澤 八水 五湖 九江 三峽 海 岱 川
澤 山水 江湖 溪澗 陂 塘波浪 源 流 潮濤 港 派
匹賣反 沙灘波瀾 汀洲 潢濱瀑布 島 嶼 溝瀦 墊橋
梁 河渡 關 津 涯 漱 浦 潢 壟 坂坡 郊 堰田 畝 岩 岬
墅 原 堯山谷 泥塗隰 阻 難狹 路 徽 徑 丘陵
塵 埃 坯上 渡口 城郭 柵頭 厈 鹵 是 僉 兵 和 四
之所 蹦 也去 危 歸 安故不 蹦 坤 利 也
士農工高 睦 五爵 公侯伯子男 故上不違
民 謂之四民 謂之五爵
天時下不蹦地利中獲人和何懽如之哉加
旗全五兵 謂之五兵 矛戈戰 安九弓
角弓 木弓 彈弓 窩弓 長弓 強弓 大弓 良弓 勁
弓謂之九弓也
趣軍退軍攻城夜衛立音

31. Ukihashi 浮橋	Raft for crossing rivers
32. Tengan 隄岸	Embankment
33. Ganshu 岩岫	A towering rock
34. Hora-ana 洞穴	A cave in rock or a cliffside
35. Horan 峰巒	The summit of a mountain
36. Enrin 園林	A grove in the middle of a garden
37. Enso 淵藪／閼藪 A place where animals gather, an area of dense foliage where an enemy might lie in wait.	
38. Kokyo 岡壠	An overlook
39. Hanpa 坂坡	A place that looks like it has been shaped by waves.
40. Kokyo 郊墟	A hill in a generally flat area
41. Sonsho 村墅	Rice field
42. Gento 原塢	A flat area in the mountains (?)
43. Sankoku 山谷	A valley
44. Deito 泥塗	A muddy road
45. Aisai 隘塞 A fortification built in peacetime to stop enemy forces at strategic points to allow you to concentrate your forces and protect the locals.	
46. Sonan 阻難	Rough, dangerous terrain
47. Sebashi 狹路	Narrow road
48. Bikei 微徑	Narrow road
49. Kyu 丘陵	Small hills
50. Ijo 圯上	Earthen bridge
51. Toko 渡口	Horses that pull boats along a river
52. Jokaku 城郭	Defenses built around a castle
53. Saku 柵頭	Top part of defensive fences
54. Sekiru 斥鹵	An area with salty soil
55. Koremina 是歛	Field
56. Tsumazuku 兵之蹶 Geographic features that make soldiers hesitate or stop their advance.	

Kokumin Yamato 国民和
All Four Social Classes of Yamato

Yamato is another name for Japan. Kuji can allow you be on good terms with any member of society, no matter what their social class. The four social classes are *Shi-no-ko-sho* 士農工商 Samurai-Farmer-Craftsmen-Merchant, which describes the four professions as well as the hierarchy in Japan.[23]

Goshaku 五爵
The Five Ranks of Nobility

You can use the Kuji to become familiar with any of the *Goshaku* 五爵 the five ranks of nobility. The five ranks refer to *Ko-Ko-Haku-Shi-Dan* 公侯伯子男 which refer to the ranks of duke, marquis, count, viscount and baron.

As for *Ten-Chi-Jin*, Heaven-Earth-Man, the most important to take advantage of is "Heaven Chance." It is imperative that you do not mistake your timing. The last thing you should consider is the terrain before you. Never hesitate no matter how dangerous the land before you. Between these two is being in harmony with people.

In other words, if you hesitate to take advantage of an opportunity, you will suddenly miss it, so a strong spirit is required.[24]

---

[23] As far as percentage of the population:
Samurai 7~10%
Farmer 80~85%
Craftsmen 4%
Merchants 4%
Also 1% priests & 1% outcasts

[24] This seems to be a variation of a line by Mencius 孟子 (372~289)
天時不如地利，地利不如人和
(Literally) *Earthly advantage is more important than heavenly time, man's harmony is more important than earthly advantage.*
(Figuratively) *In order of worthiness of consideration when planning an operation, from least to most, are weather, geography, and man's unity*

According to Zhang's commentary on Yellow Rock Old Man[25] *Rin* 臨 to Face, represents the intimidating power of the *Fuetsu* 斧鉞 or battle axe, which grants the bearer command decision.

Hyo 兵 Soldier, represents respecting the authority of soldiers to take prisoners and establish towns.

Toh 鬪 Fight, refers to the ruling family of a domain as being good stewards of the domain and enjoying the people's respect.

Sha 者 Person, refers to a reliable military commander who has unified *Sansai* 三才 the Three Powers: Heaven, Earth and Man. He employs divine timing, takes advantage of any terrain and commands in a unifying manner.

Kai 皆 Everything and Everyone, refers to focusing on the Child of Heaven, or the Emperor, who has a mandate from the gods. Regular rain means that the croups flourish. Due to a prosperous domain, the citizens do not have to worry about hunger nor cold.

Jin 陣 Legion refers to how the god of the hearth protects against fire within the camp as well as against disasters and banishes illness.

Retsu 列 to Arrange in a Line, refers to the desire to increase the number of *Sotsu* 卒, low ranking soldiers, and building a larger army thereby eliminating the possibility of defeat in battle.

Zai 在 Exist, refers to stockpiling foodstuffs as well as firewood and water. The desire to prevent your troops from becoming exhausted.

Zen 前 Before, is the desire to achieve victory without fighting. To inspire fear without having to put people to death. Your bows remain in their bags and your swords remain in their boxes. The general's will is conveyed by his ambassadors to his opponents.

---

[25] Zhang Shang Ying 張商英 (1043~1121.) Huang Shi Gong 黄石公 'Yellow Rock Old Man' is a Taoist Immortal

欲戰之不敗此在積粮食鼓薪水欲令兵
不疲勞前不戰而勝不謀而恐臺豈匱劔
將感行吏政譚リ
右九字ハ是レ太公望上世ヨリ秘懷メ
他見ヲ不許其字ノ輊ナルヲ懼レテ
其心ヲ摘テ曰テ其由所ヲ諠ブ敷歳
ノ後ニ張子房得之漢ノ世ヲ相テ興ス
之遊商英改テ書之注レ之云
前ノ一字ヲ用ユル。不戰而勝。不謀而
恐レシム。引ヲ臺ニシサメ。劔ヲ匱ニ
藏ム。上八一字ノ義ヲ一字ニ具ヘリ。故
前ノ字ヲ用トスル也ニ今前字書ノ表ニ前字足匱ノ書ス是リ

The above is how the nine Kanji that make up the Kuji were taught by the Duke Tai of Qi. This method has been kept a closely guarded secret since ancient times, and was not shown to other. The reason Duke Tai of Qi did not reveal the true meaning of these Kanji was that he was afraid of what would happen if he did.

Many years after the Duke Tai of Qi, a man Zhang Liang (251 BC ~189 BC) was taught this *Heiho* 兵法 martial arts teaching, and used it to help bring order and prosperity to the Han dynasty (202 BC ~220 AD.)

More recently Zhang Ying (1043~1121) wrote a commentary on Duke Tai of Qi's book of Military Strategy and Kuji.

Kuji With a Single Kanji

There is also a method whereby you use only the Kanji *Zen* 前 Before to represent the entirety of the Kuji. This will enable you to achieve victory without fighting. You will be able to strike fear in your enemy without having to put people to death. You can leave your bows in their bags and leave your swords stored safely in their boxes.

Since all the power of the other eight Kanji is infused into this one Kanji, you can use only the Kanji Zen. Nowadays, you see the Kanji Zen written on the front of boxes that store armor and weapons for the same reason.[26]

---

[26] Antique armor chest with the Kanji *Zen* 前 on the front.

四縱五橫傳

兵嘆論曰。專急不服、選曰。當作速用縱橫ノ
法所ニ向念七遍。畫地畢テ以三土塊ニ壓レ之便行テ
勿返顧スルニ

門
　四縱
　五橫

正立テ門内ニ叩齒三十六遍。以テ右手大姆先ツ
畫テ四縱後烏ニ五橫訖即咒曰。四縱五橫。吾
今出行。禹王衛道。蚩尤辟兵盜賊不起虎
狼不行。還歸故卿。當吾者死、背吾者亡。急
急如太上老君律令。咒畢便ケ行。慎勿ニ反顧
右ハ四豎五橫ト云是レナリ。九字ト

Yon Tate Go Yoko Den 四縱五橫傳
Drawing Four Vertical and Five Horizontal Lines.

The book *Heitanron* 兵嘆論, *Arguments Regarding Military Matters*,[27] is the first to contain a lesson regarding drawing Four Vertical and Five Horizontal Lines.

It says,

If you find yourself in a dire situation, unable to choose the day and time to perform the Kuji, you should draw the Four Vertical and Five Horizontal Lines. Face the direction you wish to travel and chant the Kuji seven times. Then draw ▦ on the ground. Once you finish the drawing, cover it with earth. Below is a diagram of how this is done

門	門	**Mon** Gate
▦	▦	
五四 ╎╎ 橫縱	五四 ╎╎ 橫縱	**Yon Tate** Four Vertical **Go Yoko** Five Horizontal

---

[27] All that is known about this book is the title. While the date and author are unknown since it is mentioned in *The Treasure Grove of Military Knowledge*, it is probably earlier than the 14th century.

Procedure

First, stand in the center of the front gate, or doorway of the place you are departing from, and clack your teeth together thirty-six times. Then use the thumb of your right hand to first draw four vertical lines followed by five horizontal lines. Immediately chant the following incantation:

I am now setting out on a journey on a path and have received divine protection. [28] *King Yu defends the way. The soldiers of Chiyou, the god of war, will avoid my path.* [29] *Thieves and robbers will find their plans fail. Tigers and wolves will not venture out to hunt. Return me to my homeland. Let those that seek to strike me perish. Let those that try to attack me from behind die. The Heavenly Lord of Dao and its Virtue should be strictly obeyed and take effect immediately.*

Once finished, you should immediately depart. Remember that you should never look back.

This ends the lesson regarding drawing Four Vertical and Five Horizontal Lines.

---

[28] *Uho* 禹歩 A ceremony performed by a sorcerer to protect a noble setting out on a trip.

[29] *Chiyou* 蚩尤 A mythical king and the Chinese god of war.

ハ別傳ナリ。然ニ四堅五横共ニ九畫能太陽ノ數ニ應ス。故ニコレヲ用ユ。九字亦然リ。是ニ因テ終ニ合セ來レリ。九ハ太陽ニメ。其勢ヒ當ルベカラズ。故ニコレヲ用ト云。豈太陽ニ勝ルモノ有シヤ。叩齒ヲ三十六遍ハ是亦太陽ノ數ナリ。四時ニ因ル九十リ。則四九ノ三十六是ナリ。大姆ヲ用ルハ大姆ハ即太陽ノ氣ノ發ルハ大姆ヨリス。氣ノ發ルハ大姆ヨリス。氣ハ即太陽ノ氣也。七遍ハ必陽ノ數ナリ。是レ皆陽德ヲ以テ身ヲ守リ敵ヲ制スルノ道ナリ。道家ニ九龍ト云ヘリ則九字ナリ。

While Kuji, the nine seals, is a separate tradition, it is important to remember that both the Four Vertical and Five Horizontal Lines as well as Kuji are written with nine strokes. This is because the number nine reflects *Taiyo no Kazu*, the Number of Greater Yang.[30]

---

[30] *Taiyo no Kazu* 太陽の数 The Number of Greater Yang (the sun) refers to *Shisho* 四象 the four phases which is part of *Ekikyo* 易経 I Ching

The four phases:
1. *Taiyo*, Greater Yang, which is comprised of Yang and Yang. Represented by Nine.
2. *Shoyo*, Lesser Yang, comprised of Yang and Yin. Represented by Seven.
3. *Shoin*, Lesser Yin, which is comprised of Yin and Yang. Represented by Eight.
4. *Taiin*, Greater Yin, which is comprised of Yin and Yin. Represented by Six.

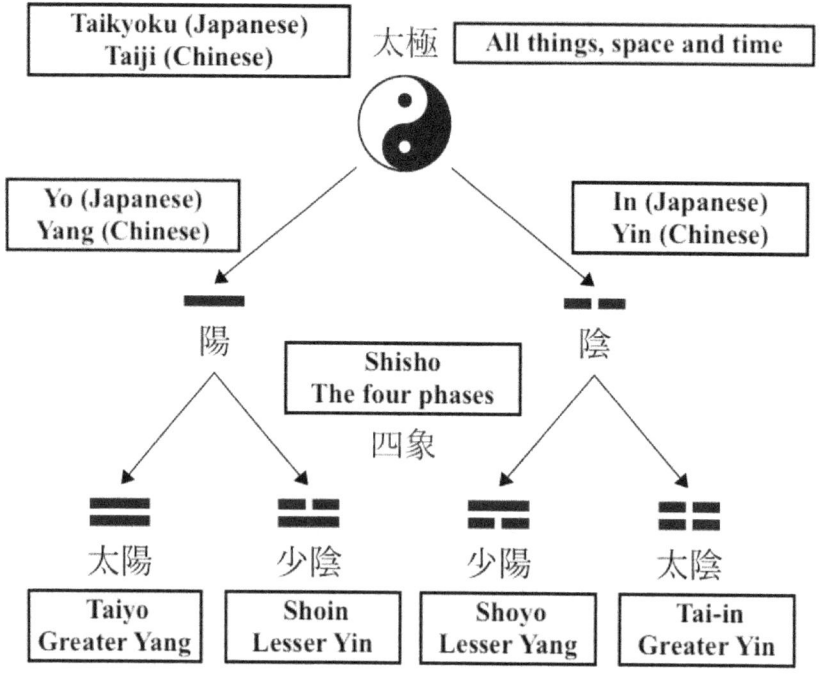

That is why both Four Vertical and Five Horizontal Lines and Kuji relate to the number nine. This is why, in the end, both of these traditions have been combined.

The number nine is used since it represents Greater Yang, the Sun, the force of which cannot be endured. How can there be anything greater than the sun?

When you clack your teeth together thirty-six times, this is also reflects the number of Greater Yang. You are combining *Shiji*, the four seasons, with nine. To achieve this, multiply the four seasons with nine, the number of Greater Yang, to arrive at a result of thirty-six. Thus, the reason you clack your teeth together thirty-six times is because you are multiplying the four seasons, spring, summer, fall and winter, with nine, which is *Taiyo-su* 太陽数, the number of Greater Yang.

As for why you draw the Four Vertical and Five Horizontal Lines with your "nursemaid finger" 大姆 or thumb is because that is where you generate your Ki, spiritual energy. Ki, spiritual energy, is the Ki of Greater Yang, represented by the Sun.

The reason you chant the Kuji seven times before drawing 丼 on the ground is because seven is the number representing Lesser Yang.

You are using the wisdom inherent in *Yotoku* 陽徳 the Virtue and Benefit of Yang, to both defend yourself and subdue your enemies. The Taoists call this the *Kyuryu* 九龍 Nine Dragons. This is referring to the Kuji, the Nine Seals.

九字佛家傳

蓋九字ハ太陽ノ秘呪トメ、全ク道家者流ノ傳ナリ。九護身法ト。九字ト。四縱五橫トハ各別ナルヲ合テ一法ニ成スフハ其元ヨル所アリ。摩利支經ニ云。日ハ天ノ所ニイテス太陽ニメ火焰天ト譯ス。或ハ陽炎天トモ譯ス。故ニ摩利支天ハ惡魔ヲ降伏シ。敵ヲ亡シ災妖毒害ヲ制スルニ。最上ノ天ナリ。是ヲ以テ武家ノ字護トス。九字ハ太公上ノ世ヨリ秘懷メ、周公ニ傳テヨリ以來、軍務ノ大事トス。則九龍ノ秘呪ニメ。太陽ノ呪ナリ。四縱

Kuji Bukkaden 九字仏家伝
How the Kuji is Used by Buddhists

The nine Kanji that make up Kuji is a secret incantation passed down by Taoist practitioners in order to invokes the power of Greater Yang. It is important to understand using the Kuji self-protection method combined with drawing the Four Vertical and Five Horizontal Lines is joining two separate traditions to create a new method.

According to the *Marishiten-kei* 摩利支経 the Sutra of Marishiten, the divine manifestation of rays of light,[31]

> *Niten, the god of the sun, is where Greater Yang can be found. It can be described as* **Kaen Ten** 火焔天 *Flaming Heaven, the main source of fire between the earth and the moon. When the flame goes upward, it is returning to this heaven.*
>
> *It is also referred to as* **Kagero Ten** 陽炎天 *Shimmering Heat Heaven, describing how waves of heat boil up.*
>
> *Thus Marishiten, as the divine incarnation of rays of light emanating from the sun, can to subdue demons, destroy enemies, and nullify natural disasters and poisonous substances.*

This is why warriors ask for the protection of Marishiten. The Kuji, a secret tradition of Duke Tai of Qi from ancient times, has passed down from Zhang Ying to become an important tool for those engaged in the art of war.

It is also known as *Kyuryu no Hiju* 九龍の秘咒 Secret Incantation of the Nine Dragons. Or *Taiyo no Ju* 太陽の咒 Greater Yang Incantation.

---

[31] It is not clear if this is the actual name of a book, or an incantation to Marishiten.

五横ハ急速用ノ法ニテ、太陽ノ符ナリ。暁天ニ向テ行フベシ。日ノ前ニイニス。摩利支天ハ日天ノ前ニイニス。太陽火焔ノモノナレバ、摩利支天ノ九字ハ。縦五横ノ九字ハ。太陽火焔ノ三昧耶形ナリ。摩利支天ノ九字ノ咒ニメ、符ハ三昧耶形ナリ。護身法ヲ九字ニメ。一切ノ法ヲ行フニ、先ヅ護身ニ附タルハ。一切ノ法ヲ以テ、三密清浄ニメ。結界ヲ成ス。故ニ法ヲ以テ、三密清浄ニメ、結界ヲ成ス。故ニ此加持力ニ依テ。其法成就ス。其上ニ被甲護身ハ。全ク摩利支ノ真言ニメ。此護身ハ。全ク摩利支ノ一體ナリ。此天ノ卯明ナリ。故ニメ。九字護身トル理ヲ以テ。三品ノ法ニス。即被甲護身号テ。摩利支天ノ秘法トス。

Kyusoku Yo 急速用
Rapid Application

Drawing the Four Vertical and Five Horizontal Lines constitutes creating a talisman that utilizes Greater Yang. The reason you face the rising sun is so you are looking directly at Marishiten, the god of rays of light who is positioned between you and Niten 二天, the sun god.

The Four Vertical and Five Horizontal Lines combined with the Kuji are channeling the fire and light of the sun, thus the incantation invokes Marishiten. The talisman you create is called *Sanmaya-Gyo* 三昧耶形 Promise Talisman. *Samaya* is a Sanskrit word meaning equality and unity while *Gyo* is a contract or talisman.

When applying the Kuji Self-Protection Method it is essential to first cleanse yourself before creating a *Kekkai* 結界 barrier ward. This cleansing is called *Sanmitsu Shojo* 三密清浄 Three Secret Purifications.[32]

Thus combining the Kuji with the Four Vertical and Five Horizontal Lines will enable you to employ the underlying forces in this prayer. This means whatever your mission may be, it will conclude successfully.

---

[32] You are purifying yourself of three sins, those of action, those of speech and those of the mind. The three Kanji that make up *Jo-Sango* 浄三業 are:

Jo 浄 Purify

San 三 Three

Go 業 Past Actions

The word "three" signifies *Shin-Ku-I* 身口意 Body- Mouth-Mind. These are each paired with the word "Past Actions" as follows:

身業 Shingo – Actions such as striking a person or killing an insect with your hands or feet.

口業 Gugo – Yelling at a person. Badmouthing a person. Spreading rumors.

意業 Igo – Thinking bad of a person or harboring hatred.

[18] Sanbu-Shoson 三部諸尊 Buddha, Bodhisattvas and Heaven.

What this means is that you are using *Hiko Goshin no Inmyo* 被甲護身の印明 a chant and mudra to enclose yourself in defensive armor. By using *Shingon*, Divine Words, and *In*, Mudra, you are invoking the protection of Marishiten.

This method combines the three virtues described above, armor, divine words, Mudra and armor into one method. It is a secret method dedicated to Marishiten, also known as *Kuji Goshin* 九字護身 Kuji for Self-Defense. With this, a Samurai can form a *Sanmaya-Gyo* 三昧耶形 Promise Talisman in order to cloak themselves in *Hiko Goshin* 被甲護身 supernatural defensive armor.

The method is as follows:
- Chant the Kuji while using the Mudra associated with each.
- Use the Immovable Sword Seal to draw the Four Vertical and Five Horizontal Lines.
- Clap while chanting *Gyo-man-boron*
- Snap your fingers three times while chanting Victory! Three times. [33]

---

[33] The author only included the names of the Kuji and the mudra used. The following illustrations and descriptions are from *Secret Method* 深秘法 by Kitazawa Yonekichi. Published in 1916.

二ッテ武士ノ三昧耶形ト成レリ

臨一外縛立ニ中、兵ニ大ニ金剛輪印
闘三外獅子印、者四内獅子印
皆五外縛印ニ大立、陣六内縛印
列七知拳印、在八日輪印
前九實施印
次ニ不動劒印ニ四ニ竪五横ニ切之

𢃇 如レ是 行曼勝
次ニ拍掌 勝三篇
次ニ彈指

Kuji – Rapid Application	
Rin 臨 **Face**	*Fugen Sanmaya-In* 普賢三昧耶印 Fugen Contract Mudra Join your left and right hands together with your fingers intertwined inside. The tips of your index fingers should be touching.
1 2 **Pyo** 兵 **Soldier**	*Daikongohrin-In* 大金剛輪印 Great Golden Wheel of Strength Seal
	1. Interlace the fingers of your right and left hands. Extend and join both index fingers together. Wrap your middle fingers over your index fingers.
	2. Starting from the Fugen Sanmaya-In, wrap the index fingers around your middle fingers.
Toh 鬪 **Fight**	*Gejishi-In* 外獅子印 Outer Lion Seal Wrap both middle fingers over both index fingers. Your thumbs, ring and little fingers should be extended with the tips touching.

 ***Sha*** 者 **Person**	*Naijishi-In* 内獅子印 Inner Lion Seal Both hands are brought together. The middle fingers wrap around the ring finger of each hand, with the index and little fingers extended. The tips of both index fingers and the tips of both little fingers are touching.
 ***Kai*** 皆 **Everything**	*Gebaku-In* 外縛印 Outer Binding Seal Bring both hands together so that the fingers cross and extend across the backs of your hands.
 ***Jin*** 陣 **Legion**	*Naibaku-In* 内縛印 Inner Binding Seal Bring all ten fingers inward so that they are together.

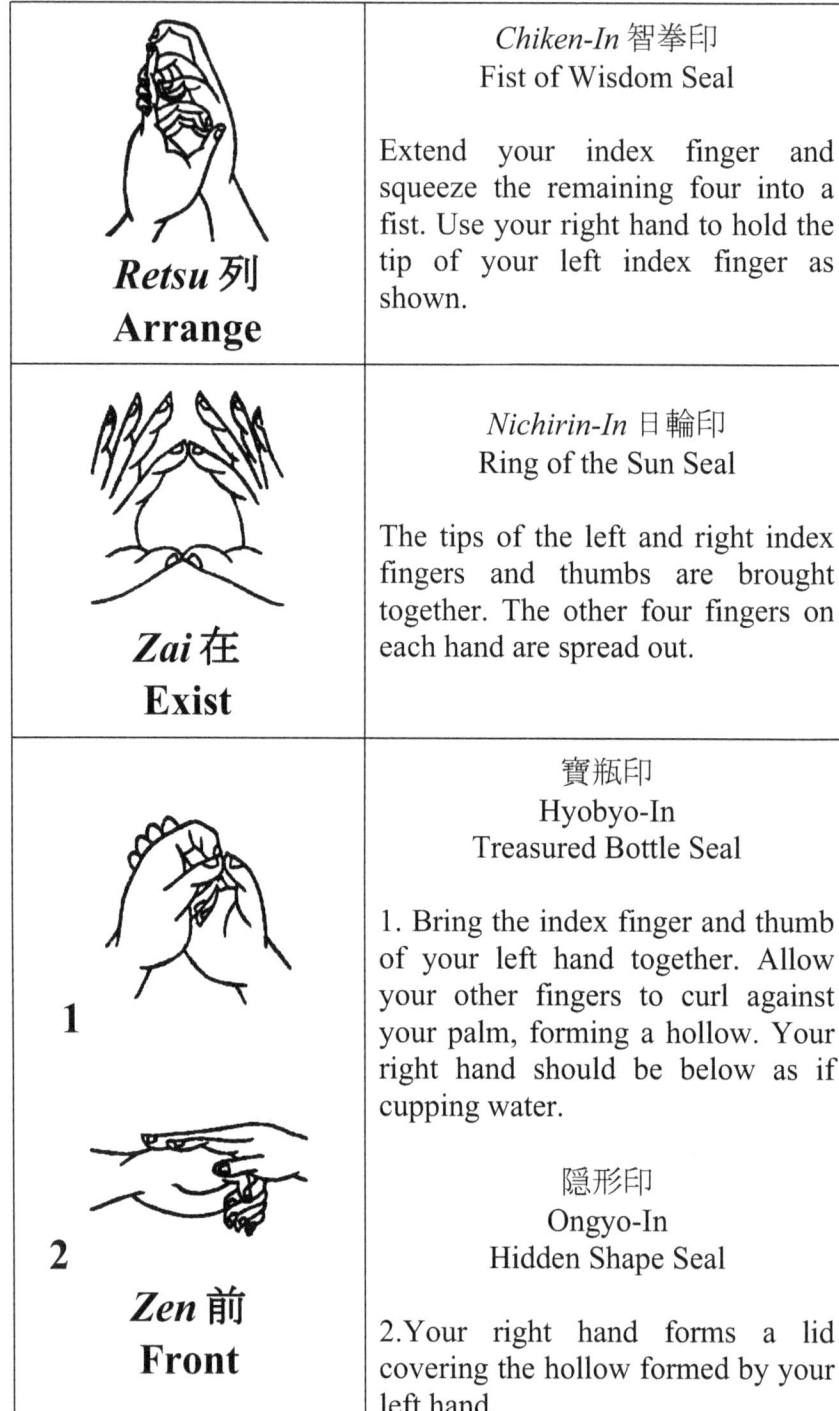

Retsu 列 Arrange

Chiken-In 智拳印
Fist of Wisdom Seal

Extend your index finger and squeeze the remaining four into a fist. Use your right hand to hold the tip of your left index finger as shown.

Zai 在 Exist

Nichirin-In 日輪印
Ring of the Sun Seal

The tips of the left and right index fingers and thumbs are brought together. The other four fingers on each hand are spread out.

Zen 前 Front

寶瓶印
Hyobyo-In
Treasured Bottle Seal

1. Bring the index finger and thumb of your left hand together. Allow your other fingers to curl against your palm, forming a hollow. Your right hand should be below as if cupping water.

隱形印
Ongyo-In
Hidden Shape Seal

2. Your right hand forms a lid covering the hollow formed by your left hand.

Use the Immovable Sword Seal to draw the Four Vertical and Five Horizontal Lines

Use your right hand to make the *Fudo Ken-in* 劍印 Immovable Sword Seal and cut the Four Vertical and Five Horizontal Lines.

Illustrations from *Kuji* by Fujita Seiko 1963. Fujita Seiko uses the word *Toh-in* Katana Seal instead of *Ken-in* Sword Seal. This is also called Immovable Seal.	
1. Form the sword seal, with your right and the scabbard with your left.	2. Insert the sword into the scabbard.
刀印	
3. Holding your hands by your left side, draw the sword seal.	4. After drawing the sword from the sheath, cut in the prescribed pattern.
	刀印
	Yon Tate Four Vertical **Go Yoko** Five Horizontal

Hakusho 拍掌 Clapping

Next, while clapping chant *Gyo-man-boron*[34] 行曼勝

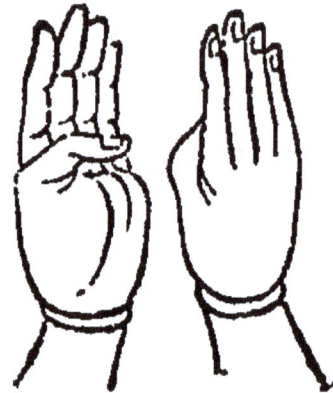

Tanji 弾指 Snapping Your Fingers

Next, snap your fingers and chant three times. This is done by first pressing your thumb on top of your index finger. Then snap your index finger outward, making a snapping sound.

This is the end of the section dealing with how Kuji is transmitted in Buddhism. The Kuji, nine seals, each have a mudra and, when combined with chanting sacred words, are known as the Kuji fulfillment ceremony.

---

[34] The meaning of this is unknown.

右ハ佛家ヨリ傳ル所ナリ。各〻卯明ヲ
附ダル故ニ、九字成就ノ式ト云。是ニ
亦或ハ真言比丘ノ傳ヲ記ス。參考ニ具
ルモノナリ

臨　多門天　　　　　寶瓶卯 外縛〆揩
兵　降三世　　　　　大金剛輪卯
闘　持國天　　　　　閃獅子卯
者　金剛夜叉　　　　外獅子卯
皆　大聖不動　　　　外縛大ニ立風合
陣　軍荼利　　　　　内縛卯
列　廣目天　　　　　知拳卯

Shingon Biku no Den 真言比丘
Shingon Monk Transmission

There is an additional method called *Shingon Biku no Den* 真言比丘 Shingon Monk Transmission.[35]

Kuji *Shingon Biku no Den* 真言比丘 Shingon Monk Transmission

Invoking: *Tamonten* 多聞天 All-Hearing King
Mudra: *Hyobyo-In* 寶瓶印 Treasured Bottle Seal

Join your left and right hands together with your fingers intertwined inside. The tips of your index fingers should be touching.

---

[35] The author only included the names of the Kuji and the mudra used. The illustrations of the Mudra are from:
Secret Method 深秘法 by Kitazawa Yonekichi. Published in 1916.
The illustrations of the dieties being invoked are from:
An Illustrated Guide to Buddhist Deities 仏像図彙 By Tosa Hidenobu 土佐秀信 Published 1900. Based on book from 1690.

Pyo 兵 **Soldier**	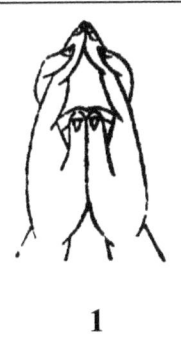 1	 2	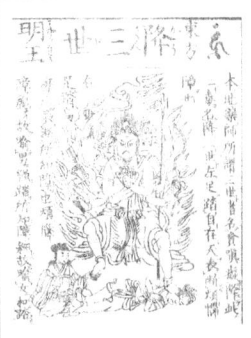

Invoking: *Gozanze Myo-o* 降三世明王 Gozanze Wisdom King
Mudra: *Daikongohrin-In* 大金剛輪印
Great Golden Wheel of Strength Seal

1. Interlace the fingers of your right and left hands. Extend and join both index fingers together. Wrap your middle fingers over your index fingers.

2. Starting from the Fugen Sanmaya-In, wrap the index fingers around your middle fingers.

Toh 鬭 **Fight**		

Invoking: *Jikokuten* 持國天 Upholder of the Nation King

Mudra: *Naijishi-In* 內獅子印 Inner Lion Seal

Wrap both middle fingers over both index fingers. Your thumbs, ring and little fingers should be extended with the tips touching.

| *Sha* 者 **Person** |  | 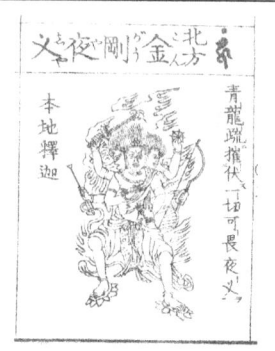 |

Invoking: *Kongoyasha Myo-o* 金剛夜叉明王
Kongoyasha Wisdom King

Mudra: *Gejishi-In* 外獅子印 Outer Lion Seal

Both hands are brought together. The middle fingers wrap around the ring finger of each hand, with the index and little fingers extended. The tips of both middle fingers and the tips of both little fingers are touching.

| *Kai* 皆 **Everything** | 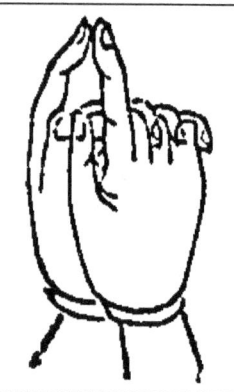 |  |

Invoking: *Taisei Myo-o* 大聖不動 Taisei Wisdom King

Mudra: *Gebaku-In* 外縛印 Outer Binding Seal

Bring both hands together so that the fingers cross and extend across the backs of your hands. Your index fingers and thumbs should be raised.

Jin 陣 **Legion**

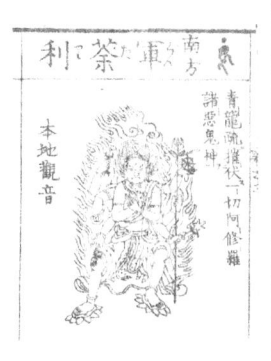

Invoking: *Gundari Myo-o* 軍荼利明王 Gundari Wisdom King

Mudra: *Naibaku-In* 内縛印 Inner Binding Seal

Bring all ten fingers inward so that they are together.

Retsu 列 **Arrange**

Invoking: *Komokuten* 広目 Wide Eyed King

Mudra: *Chiken-In* 智拳印 Fist of Wisdom Seal

Extend your index finger and squeeze the remaining four into a fist. Use your right hand to hold the tip of your left index finger as shown.

| *Zai* 在 Exist |  |  |

Invoking: *Daiitoku Myo-o* 大威徳明王 Daiitoku Wisdom King

Mudra: *Nichirin-In* 日輪印 Ring of the Sun Seal

The tips of the left and right index fingers and thumbs are brought together. The other four fingers on each hand are spread out.

| *Zen* 前 Front |   |  |

Invoking: *Zohjoten* 増長天 Increasing King

Mudra: *Ongyo-In* 隠形印 Hidden Shape Seal

1. Bring the index finger and thumb of your left hand together. Allow your other fingers to curl against your palm, forming a hollow. Your right hand should be below as if cupping water.

2. Your right hand forms a lid covering the hollow formed by your left hand.

This is also known as *Hyobyo-In* 寶瓶印 Treasured Bottle Seal

Method Taught by an Ajari 阿闍梨 a high-level Buddhist priest

The following illustration show a secret Kuji self-defense spell to create a protective ward. It was taught to me by an Ajari 阿闍梨 high Buddhist priest.

Method Taught by an Ajari 阿闍梨 a high-level Buddhist priest.
Illustrated Explanation of Interactions
The Kuji Kanji and the Deity Invoked
(Original)

説圖

東

鬭 天國持	兵 世三降	臨 天門多
者 叉夜副金	皆 動不聖大	陣 利蔡軍
前 天長増	在 德威大	列 天目廣

西

北

南

在 大威德 前 増長天

日輪卯 陰形卯 宝瓶卯

SECRETS OF THE KUJI・九字秘傳

Method Taught by an *Ajari* 阿闍梨 a high-level Buddhist priest.
Illustrated Explanation of Interactions
The Kuji Kanji and the Deity Invoked
(Transcript)

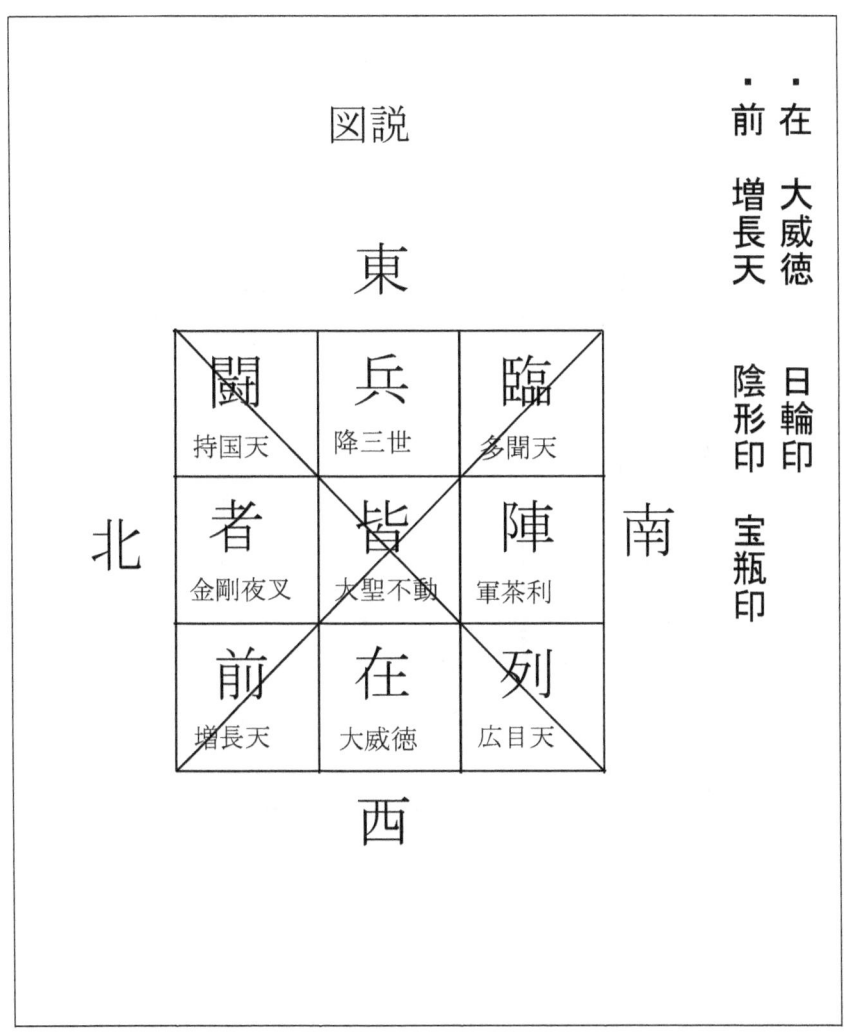

Method Taught by an Ajari 阿闍梨 a high-level Buddhist priest.
Illustrated Explanation of Interactions
The Kuji Kanji and the Deity Invoked
(Kanji/English)

East 東

鬪	兵	臨
Jikokuten 持国天	gouzanze 降三世	Tamonten 多聞天
者	皆	陣
Kongouyasha 金剛夜叉	Daishofudou 大聖不動	Gundari 軍荼利
前	在	列
Zochoten 増長天	Daiitoku 大威徳	Koumokuten 広目天

North 北 — South 南

West 西

SECRETS OF THE KUJI • 九字秘傳

Method Taught by a high-level Buddhist priest
Illustrated Explanation of Interactions
The Kuji Kanji and the Deity Invoked
(English)

East

Fight Upholder of the Nation King	**Soldier** Conqueror of three worlds Wisdom King	**Face** All-Hearing King
Person All-Penetrating Wisdom King	**Everyone** Great Honored Immovable Wisdom King	**Legion** Destroyer of Sickness Wisdom King
Before Increasing King	**Exist** Destroyer of Death Wisdom King	**Assemble** Wide-Eyed King

North (left) — **South** (right)

South

Method Taught by an Ajari 阿闍梨 a high-level Buddhist priest.
Illustrated Explanation of Interactions of Directions, Seasons, Intervals Between Seasons as well as the Kuji and the Deity Invoked (Original)

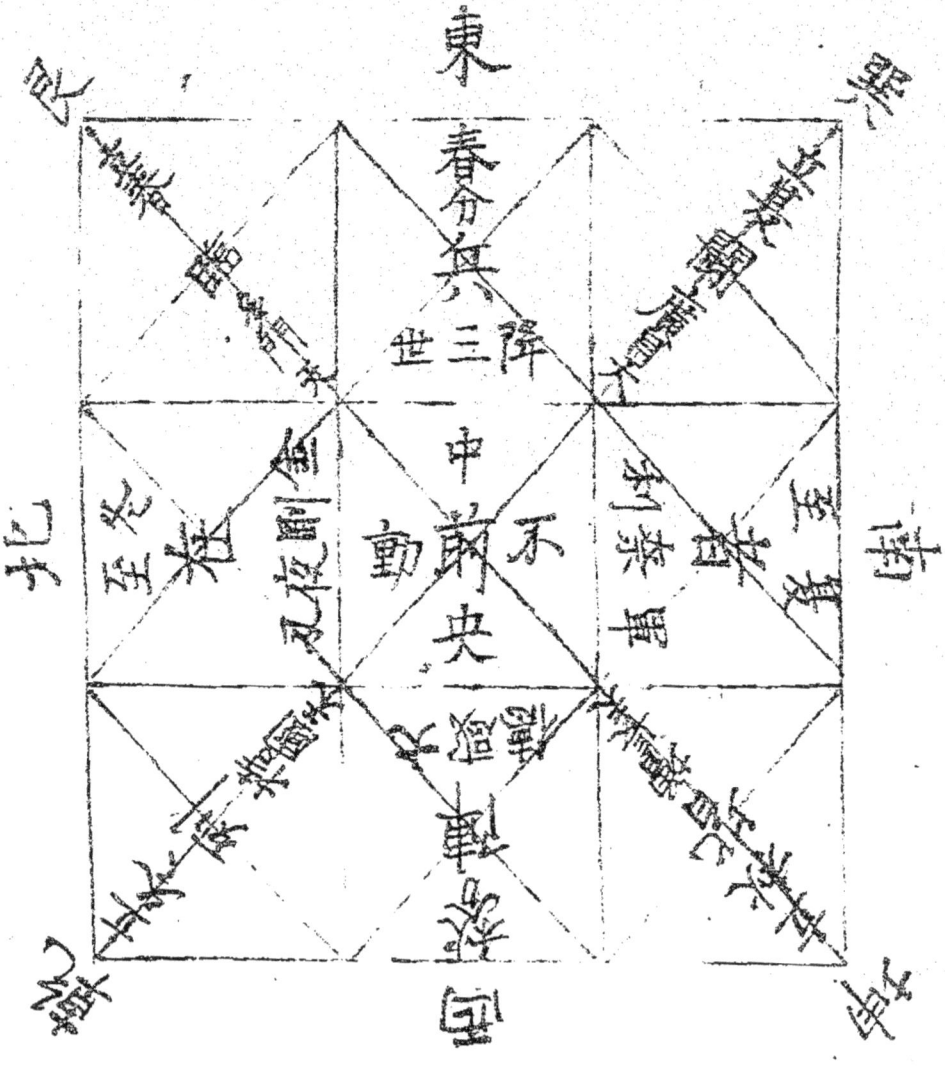

Method Taught by an Ajari 阿闍梨 a high-level Buddhist priest.
Illustrated Explanation of Interactions of Directions, Seasons, Intervals Between Seasons as well as the Kuji and the Deity Invoked
(Transcription)

図説

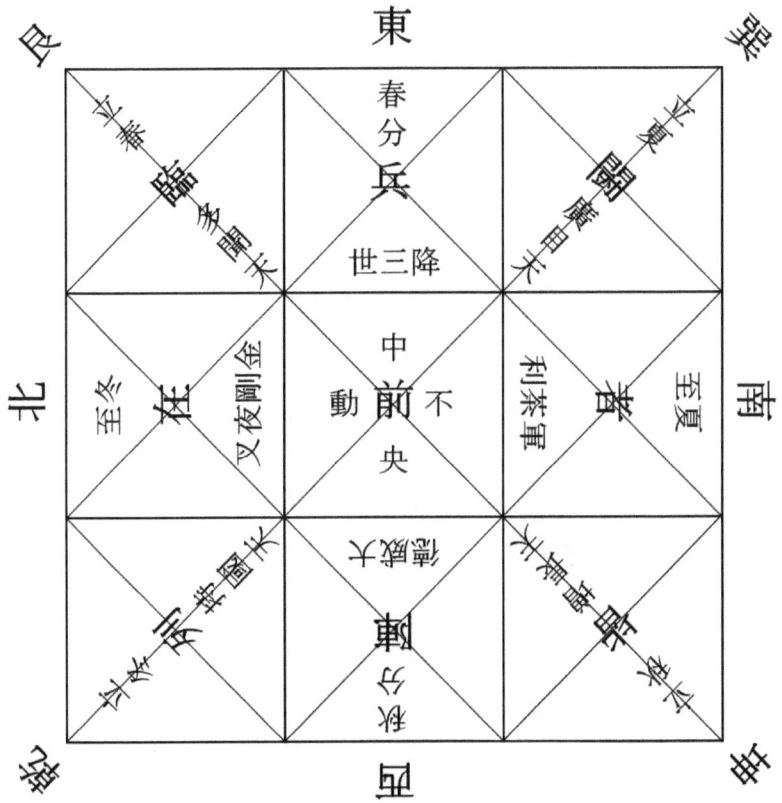

Method Taught by an Ajari 阿闍梨 a high-level Buddhist priest.
Illustrated Explanation of Interactions of Directions, Seasons, Intervals Between Seasons as well as the Kuji and the Deity Invoked (Kanji/ English)

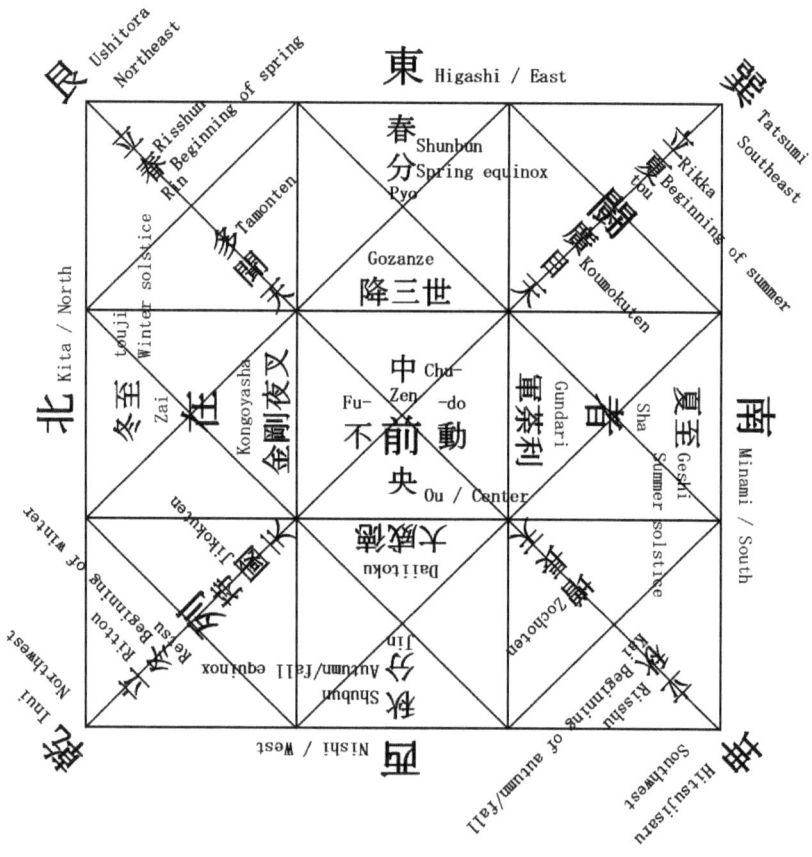

SECRETS OF THE KUJI・九字秘傳

<u>Method Taught by an Ajari 阿闍梨 a high-level Buddhist priest.</u>
Illustrated Explanation of Interactions of Directions, Seasons, Intervals Between Seasons as well as the Kuji and the Deity Invoked (English)

	Illustrated Explanation of Interactions The Kuji Kanji and the Deity Invoked	
Northeast Mountain	East	Southeast Wind
North — First day of Spring **Rin** All-Hearing King	Spring Equinox **Pyo** Conqueror of the three worlds Wisdom King	First day of Summer **Toh** Upholder of the Nation King — South
Shortest day **Jin** Destroyer of Sickness Wisdom King	Center **Sha** All-Penetrating Wisdom King	Longest day **Kai** Great Honored Immovable Wisdom King
First day of Winter **Retsu** Wide-Eyed King	Autumnal Equinox **Zen** Increasing King	First day of autumn **Zai** Destroyer of Death Wisdom King
Northwest Heaven	West	Southwest Earth

69

右ハ護身結界ノ九字トテ。阿闍梨ヨリ秘ニ授スル所ナリ。此外ニ猶亦金剛結界護身ノ九字トテ。極秘傳トスルアリ。是ニ記ス

一 外縛卯　兵ニ内縛卯
三 外縛卯　闘四内縛卯
五 外縛卯　者六内縛卯
七 外縛卯　陣八内縛卯
九 外縛卯　在
前九 聖不動結界護身卯
　　　　　右手ノ劔卯ニ如圖切レ之也。中ノ
臨兵者十前列　一者中央不動之点也
　　十　十
　　在　列

Kongo Kekkai Goshin no Kuji 金剛結界護身の九字
Kuji for creating an Iron-Strong Self-Defense Ward

There are other secret Kuji methods to create iron-strong self-defense wards around yourself. This method uses only three Mudra.

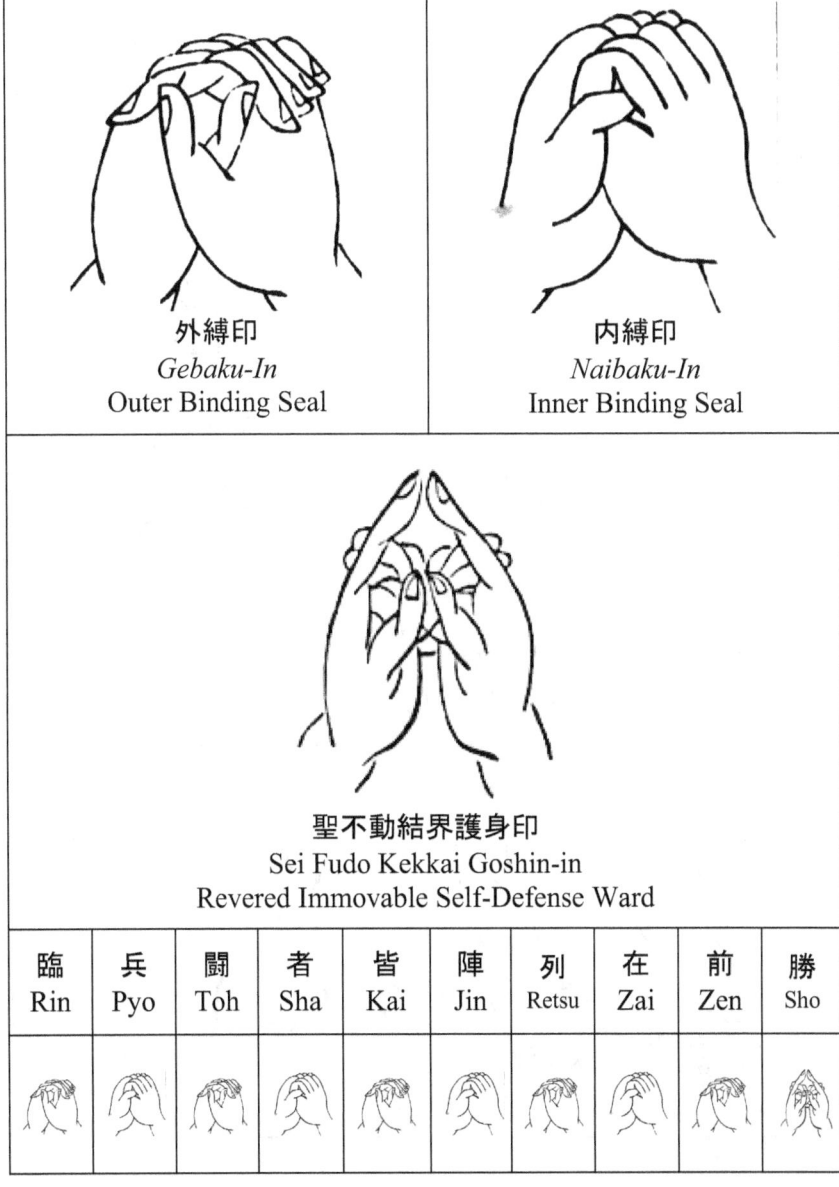

外縛印
Gebaku-In
Outer Binding Seal

内縛印
Naibaku-In
Inner Binding Seal

聖不動結界護身印
Sei Fudo Kekkai Goshin-in
Revered Immovable Self-Defense Ward

臨	兵	鬪	者	皆	陣	列	在	前	勝
Rin	Pyo	Toh	Sha	Kai	Jin	Retsu	Zai	Zen	Sho

After chanting the Kuji with the above Mudra, next use your right hand to make the *Ken-in* 劔印 sword seal.

Kuji-Kiri 九字切 Cutting the Nine Seals With the Sword Seal Illustrations from *Kuji* by Fujita Seiko 1963. Fujita Seiko uses the word *Toh-in* Katana Seal instead of *Ken-in*.	
1. Form the sword seal, with your right and the scabbard with your left.	2. Insert the sword into the scabbard.
刀印	刀印
3. Holding your hands by your left side, draw the sword seal.	4. After drawing the sword from the sheath, cut in the prescribed pattern.
	刀印

To create the *Sei Fudo Kekkai Goshin-in* 聖不動結界護身印 Revered Immovable Self-Defense Ward. First draw the Sword Seal, as described on the previous page and cut as shown in the diagram below. The final cut, a stab to the center, representing *Zen* 前 Before, is infused with the power of Fudo Myo-o, Lord of Light.

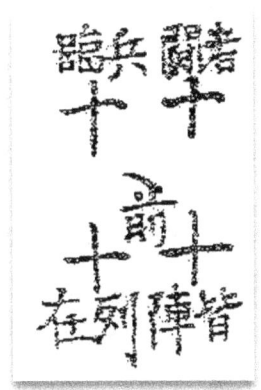

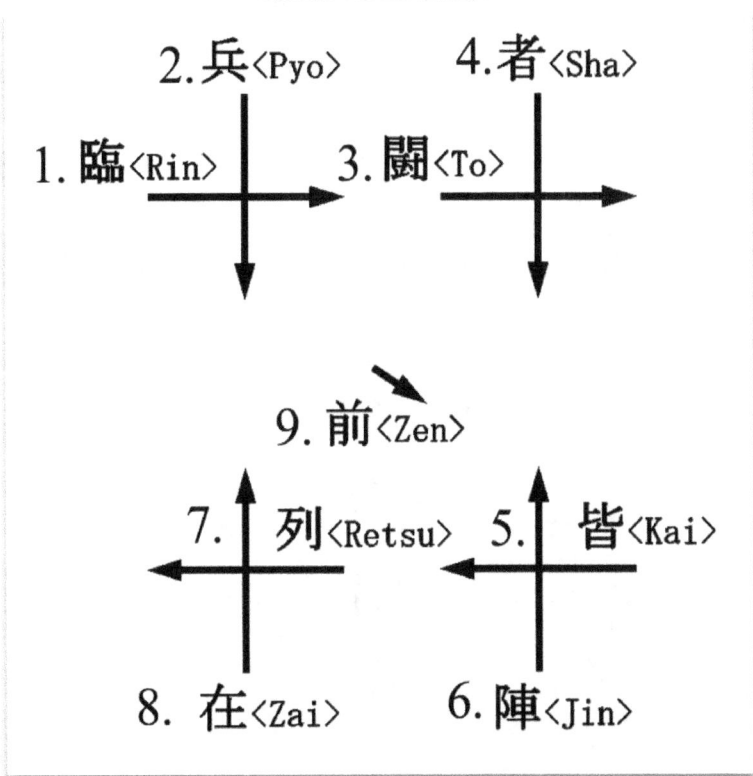

右前ノ結界ノ九字ト圖説同意ナリ。
此ニ法ハ其本不動結界ノ法也。故ニ
前ノ字ニ至テ不動ノ卯ヲ用テ結界
ヲ成ナリ圖ヲ按ズベシ。亦摩利支天
九字ノ大事ト云ナリ。是ニ記ス

・外獅子卯　臨兵關者皆陣列在前勝
・内獅子卯　唵摩利支曳娑婆訶
・馬頭卯
・日輪故光卯　南無日輪摩利支天娑婆
　　訶　三遍　　　　臨兵闘者皆陣列在レ前
・陰形卯明　唵旋陀羅耶甲集息災安穩

I have introduced two methods here. The first was a series of illustrations to create a secret Kuji self-defense spell to create a protective ward that was taught to me by an Ajari 阿闍梨 high Buddhist priest. The following method taught how to create iron-strong self-defense wards around yourself. The purpose of these methods is the same.

The fundamental purpose of these methods is to create a *Fudo Kekkai* 不動結界 immovable barrier. Therefore, for those techniques, while chanting the Kuji starting at Rin and proceeding all the way to Zen, you are using *Fudo no In*, Immovable Seal. Meaning they are dedicated to Fudo, the lord of light who represents immovable wisdom. Using these mudra with the Kuji will enable you to form an immovable boundary barrier.

There is also a teaching about a Marishiten Kuji. This will be described next.

Marishiten Kuji no Daiji 摩利支天九字の大事
How to Use the Kuji Dedicated to Marishiten

Form Outer Lion Seal and chant the Kuji, adding the Kanji *Sho* 勝 victory, to the end.

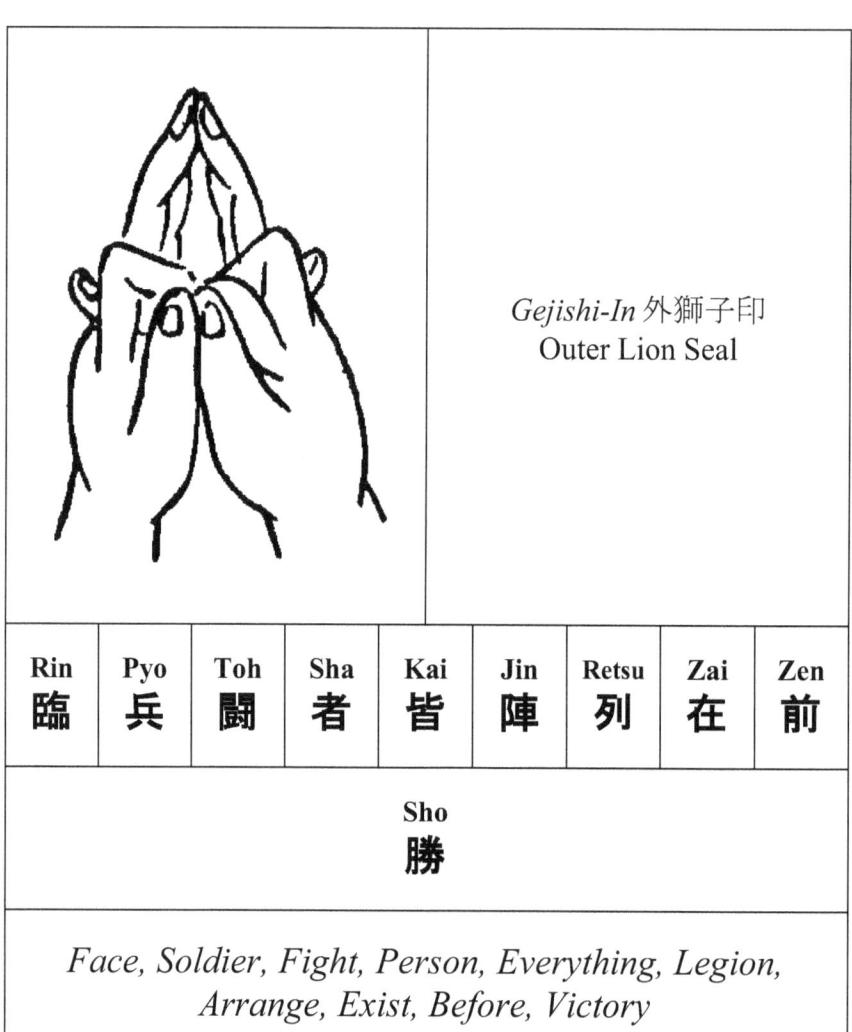

Gejishi-In 外獅子印
Outer Lion Seal

Rin	Pyo	Toh	Sha	Kai	Jin	Retsu	Zai	Zen
臨	兵	闘	者	皆	陣	列	在	前

Sho
勝

Face, Soldier, Fight, Person, Everything, Legion, Arrange, Exist, Before, Victory

Next form the Inner Lion Seal and chant the following,

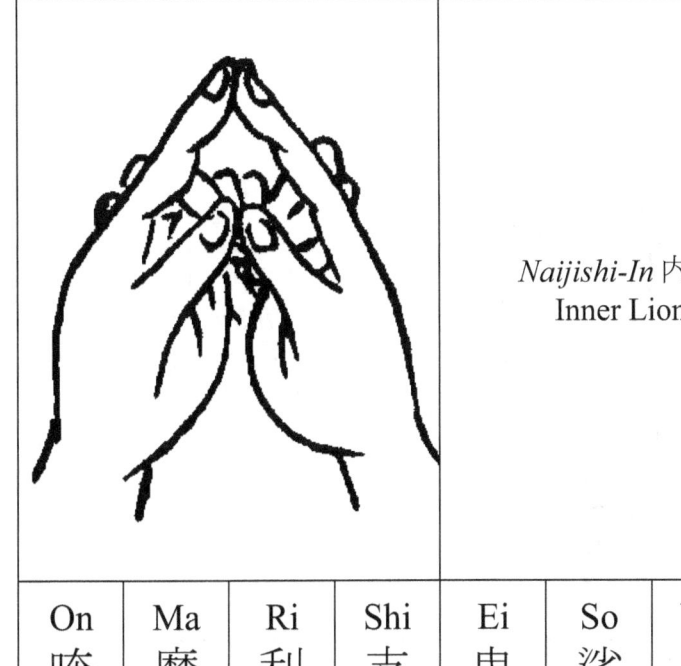

Naijishi-In 內獅子印
Inner Lion Seal

On	Ma	Ri	Shi	Ei	So	Wa	Ka
唵	摩	利	支	曳	娑	婆	訶

オンマリシエイソワカ
Chant: *On Marishi Ei Sowaka*
Meaning: *I will call your name anywhere and everywhere, please grant me your protection.*

Then form the Seal of Batto, the Horse Headed Wisdom King, who is a wrathful emanation of Kannon. Chant the following incantation. In this incantation the Kanji Zen is placed before Zai and the entire Kuji sentence takes on a slightly different meaning.

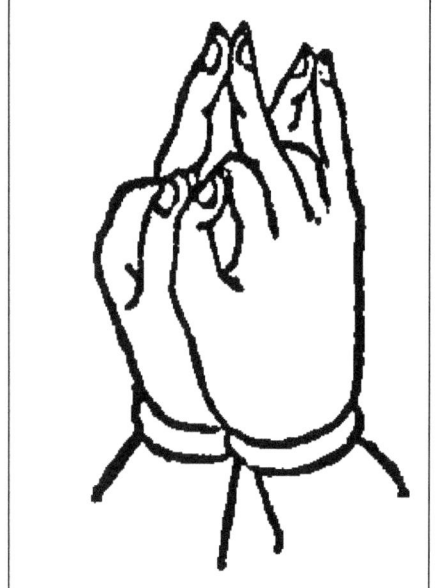

馬頭印
Batto-In
Seal of the Horse Headed Wisdom King

Rin	Pyo	Toh	Sha	Kai	Jin	Retsu	Zen	Zai
臨	兵	闘	者	皆	陣	列	前	在

「臨める兵(つわもの)、闘う者、皆陣列(やぶ)れて前に在り

When facing a powerful Tsuwamono, soldier, those that seek to fight, all break out from the ranks and move to the vanguard.

Next, chant the following three times while making Ring of the Sun Seal.

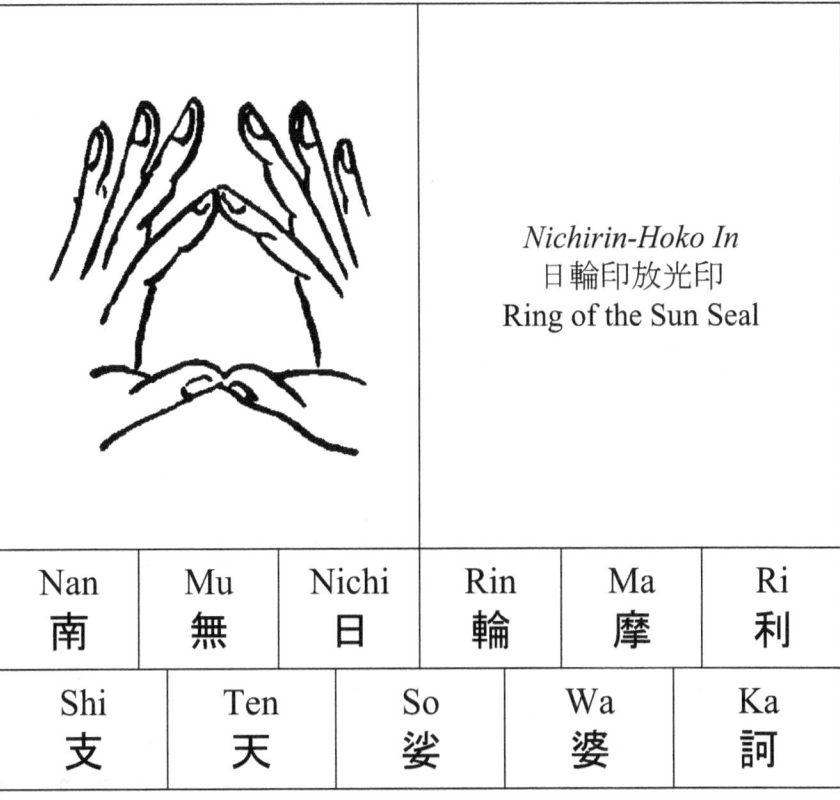

Nichirin-Hoko In
日輪印放光印
Ring of the Sun Seal

Nan 南	Mu 無	Nichi 日	Rin 輪	Ma 摩	Ri 利
Shi 支	Ten 天	So 娑	Wa 婆	Ka 訶	

Chant: *Nanmu Nichirin Marishiten Sowaka*
Meaning: *Praise Nichirin, the Sun, and Marishiten, the rays of light, please grant me your protection.*

Finally, form the Secret Shape Binding seal and chant the following three times. Then cut the Four Vertical and Five Horizontal Lines.

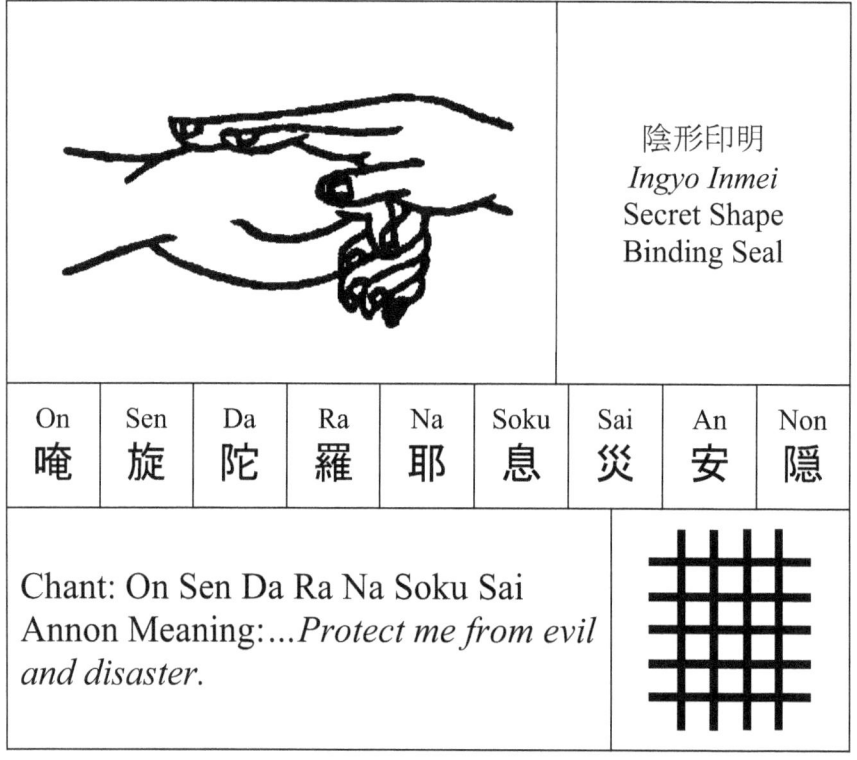

陰形印明
Ingyo Inmei
Secret Shape
Binding Seal

On	Sen	Da	Ra	Na	Soku	Sai	An	Non
唵	旋	陀	羅	耶	息	災	安	隱

Chant: On Sen Da Ra Na Soku Sai Annon Meaning:....*Protect me from evil and disaster.*

隱形三遍 䡾 四一竪 五一横

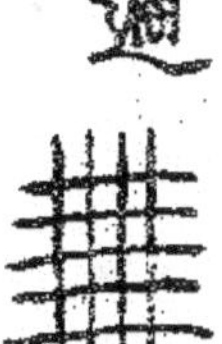

右ノ外ニ傳法數ノ多クアリ。其品悉クハ
記シ難シ。故ニ畧シ之者也
法華ノ妙ノ九ノ字ト云アリ。日蓮宗ノ輩
傳之。是相擬々作意シタル者也。是ニ
記ノ共傳ルモノナリ

妙法蓮華經序品第一
九ノ字也

妙
九ノ畫ニ切レ之。赤四ノ竪五ノ横ヲモ
切ノ之十リ

There are many other traditions besides ones described above. It is difficult to describe them all, so the rest will be abbreviated.

Hoge no Myo Kuji 法華の妙九字
The Use of Mysterious as a Kuji Found in the Lotus Sutra

Secret Kuji are described in the Lotus Sutra. This is a legend passed down in the Nichiren Sect of Buddhism. It is however a rather quaint imitation of the original Kuji and the Four Vertical and Five Horizontal Lines.

The Kuji is called:

Myoho-renge-kyo Johon Dai Ichi Kuji 妙法蓮華経序品第一九字
The Number One Kuji of the Mysterious Lotus Sutra

This method uses the Kanji Myo 妙 meaning mysterious, however additional strokes have been added to the Kanji in order to make the Kanji have nine cuts.

Left: The Kanji Myo with nine strokes from the text.
Center: The standard way to write Myo
Right: Order of the nine cuts to draw the Kanji Myo.

By cutting the Kanji Myo in this fashion, means it can invoke the same supernatural power as drawing the Four Vertical and Five Horizontal Lines.

立春大吉ト書事即春ノ字九畫ニ〆
九字ニ中ルルナリ。峽ノ字ノ如シ此類
赤多クアリ。家々ニ秘セリ。兵家者流
ニ別メ品アリ。後ニ大ノ暑記之ヲ、
兵家者流ノ秘傳スル所。佛家ヨリ傳
來ノモノアリ。亦一家ノ秘授アリ。亦
發明ノ術アリ。其類盡スベカラズ。故
ニ大ノ暑ヲ記シ置者ナリ
ニ記ス所ノ品々ニ因テ。其法ヲ
化前ニ記ス所無シ。故ニ前ニ飯メ再ビ
立ザルモノ多シ。各合セ看テ察スベシ。
セザル所多シ。
精ク八九字秘解ニ具フ

Regarding the Kanji Haru, or Spring in the Phrase *Risshun Daikichi* 立春大吉 Great Luck on the First Day of Spring

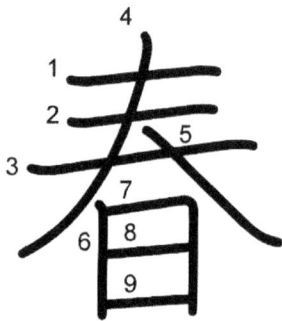

The Kanji *Haru* 春 spring, is also pronounced Shun. This Kanji is normally written with nine strokes, therefore it is related to Kuji. It is similar to the previously mentioned alternate form of the Kanji Myo, mysterious written with nine strokes as shown in the illustration below.

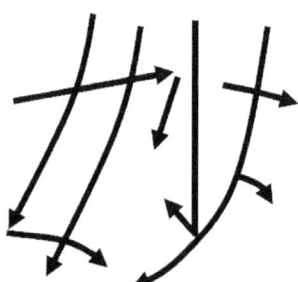

There are many different kinds of secret Kanji like this that are only passed down within the school of Taoism, Buddhism or martial arts from where they originate.

The Kuji traditions handed down in martial arts families are different from those handed down in the Nichiren Sect of Buddhism. These will be discussed in the following section.

The Kuji traditions handed down in martial arts families actually originated in Buddhism. Each family then handed down the tradition from generation to generation. In addition many schools develop their own techniques. These methods are so numerous that it would be impossible to catalogue them all. Thus, this book will only include an outline of these techniques.

None of the examples that follow contain methods that were not mentioned before. Therefore, as the methods were explained before I will not go back to the aforementioned places and explain them again. I will leave it up to the reader to compare the relevant sections and infer their meaning.

For a more detailed analysis, please see *Kuji Hikai* 九字秘解 Secrets of Kuji Explained.[36]

---

[36] This appears to be another book by the same author.

九字兵家傳

兵ハ身ニ具ヲナシテ、敵ヲ制スルナリ。
孔歇ヲ行フニ刀劔ヲ以テス。是一人ノ働キ
ナリ。ヘ雖其能スルニ至テス。
欺ヘシ。故ニ武士タル者ノ大敵ヲ專務ナリ。
匹夫ヨリ上將ニ至ルマデ知ラザルニ力
キハ身必ズ危カルベキナリ。
劔ハ只能切ヲ以テ用トス。古
神佛ノ力ヲタノミテ豈咒ノ唱ヘ
不文ニメ書ニ著スコト不能。故ニ此道ノ術ノ者
僧ニ因ル。是ニ於テ皆佛道ニ理ヲ取ル
是ヲ以テ其附會轉傳セリ。然レ圧心ヲ

Kuji Heikaden 九字兵家傳
The Sword Fighter's Guide to Kuji

Soldiers are men who control the enemy with their weapons. For the most part, soldier use edged weapons to strike the enemy. While this is how you would deal with one person, you must also be able to defeat a multitude of opponents. Therefore, every warrior has an obligation to learn the Sword Fighter's Guide to Kuji. This includes not only high-ranked soldiers but also low ranked. If you are not initiated into this art, you are in danger.

However the sword, spears and halberds are only tools used for cutting. How can a Samurai use a mantra to ask for the power of the gods and Buddha?[37] Long ago warriors were often unable to read or write particularly well, so they would have been unable to copy the lessons down. Thus, the origins of Kuji are attributed to learned monks. Samurai later adopted the method based on what Buddhist monks taught them. Therefore, when warriors first learned the Kuji, they contained the principles Buddhism. Those teachings were then passed on from one generation to the next.

---

[37] Invoking both Shinto deities as well as Buddhist deities.

正クスルヲ丁助ナキニ非。夫心正シテ道亦正シ。道正メ法術亦正シ。能正キヲ以テ邪ヲ制ス。豈不勝ノ義アラニヤ。然バ用テ盆ナルニハ去ベカズ。其ノ正ヲ選テ取ベキナリ。就中九字ハ兵家ノモノナレバ信メ用ベキナリ。其傳卯明アルニ因テ。佛家ヨリ受來ル。亦一家ノ發明ナド。各一ニアラズ。真ニ合モノヲ選用ベシ。本九字ト稱ズルモノ前ニ書ス所ノ佛家傳是ナリ。清浄之早九字。不動ノ卯明ヲ用。次ニ右手ノ劔ノ卯ニ切レ之。

However, if you do not have a spirit which is straight and true, this method will be of no use to you. When the mind is right, the way is also right. If the way is right, then the technique will also be right. By doing what is right, you will be able to conquer evil. How can a person who follows this doctrine be defeated? Thus, it should never be used to enrich yourself. You must choose the right way and only apply it to reach that goal.

Since Kuji is a technique used in military strategy, particularly swordfighting, it is something that can be trusted. Further, as it also contains *Inmyo*, mudras combined with incantations, which means that the teachings have been handed down from Buddhist practitioners.

It is important to note that Kuji were not the invention of a single group, nor can they be said to be unique to one group or another. Therefore you must choose the one that truly fits your needs and abilities. Another way to refer to the *Bukke Den* 佛家傳 Buddhist Kuji Tradition is *Hon Kuji* 本九字 Primary Kuji.

四竪
五横

臨兵闘者皆陣列在前

勝勝勝　拍掌

吽　　　彈指

右早九字ト云。不動印ハ結東十リ。其
剱印右ノ手ヲ以テ直ニ四ノ縱五ノ横ニ切
ッ架シ右ノ圖ノ且コレヲ早九字ト云ヒテ
別ニ清浄之早九字ト云アリ

十　竪横二切臨前　不動印

Seijo no Haya Kuji 清浄之早九字
The Purifying Fast Kuji

This uses the *Fudo Inmyo* 不動印明 Immovable Seal and Sacred Words. First, make the Immovable Seal, with your right-hand in the Ken-in, sword symbol, you make the following cuts.

Form a sword and scabbard with your hands. Draw the *Ken-in* 劔印, sword seal, from the scabbard and draw the Four Horizontal and Five Vertical Lines while chanting the Kuji.

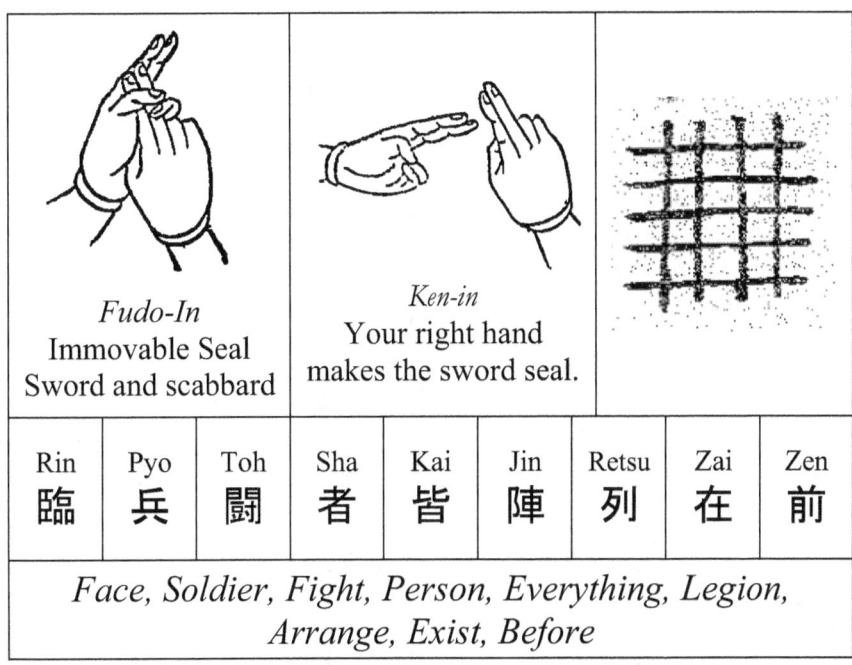

Rin	Pyo	Toh	Sha	Kai	Jin	Retsu	Zai	Zen
臨	兵	闘	者	皆	陣	列	在	前

Face, Soldier, Fight, Person, Everything, Legion, Arrange, Exist, Before

Then clap three times while chanting *Sho* 勝, victory, three times. After that snap your fingers while chanting 吽 Om/Aun, a syllable representing the primordial trinity of Vishnu, Shiva and Brahma.

The above is what is referred to as *Haya Kuji*, Fast Nine Seals. The *Fudo-In*, Immovable Seal, creates a protective ward around you.

This technique is also known as *Haya Kuji*, Rapid Nine Seals. However there is a separate technique called *Seijo no Haya Kuji*, Purifying Rapid Nine Seals.

行清勝

唵婆婆訶　一遍
紛舍克　掌内三度誦
吃吃吃　拍手
　　　　彈指

右先ニ不動ノ仰次ニ直ニ右ヘ手ヲ𨫤仰ニテ切ナリ。之ヲ清淨之早九ノ字ト云

勝勝勝　是ヲ唱ヘ、兩ノ手ヲ以テ空ヲツカム。之ヲ亦早九ノ字ト云

前　一字ノ九ノ字ト云。觀念ナリ

Seijo no Haya Kuji 清浄之早九字
Purifying Rapid Nine Seals

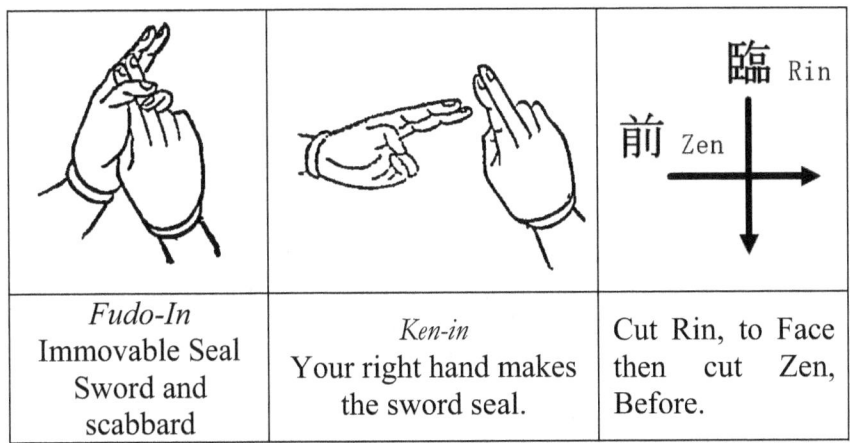

Fudo-In Immovable Seal Sword and scabbard	*Ken-in* Your right hand makes the sword seal.	Cut Rin, to Face then cut Zen, Before.

Begin by making the *Fudo-in* 不動印, Immovable Seal, then drawing Ken-in, Sword Seal, and making two cuts: *Rin* 臨 to Face, and *Zen* 前 Before. These are the first and last Kanji of the Kuji.

Next, chant *Gyo Man Sho* 行滿(満)勝 one time.

Then chant *Aum, Sowaka* 唵娑婆訶[38] "Let it be said," three times into your palm.

After that, Chant *Nayakoku* 納舎克 while clapping.

Finally, chant Om/Aun 吽吽吽 a syllable representing the primordial trinity of Vishnu, Shiva and Brahma, three times while snapping your fingers.

This is what is known as *Seijo no Haya Kuji*, Purifying Fast Nine Seals.[39]

---

[38] *Sowaka* 娑婆訶 marks the end of a mantra.

[39] Matsuda Sadakata's *Encyclopedia of Secret Methods* 妙術秘法大全 describes using this method to stop an attacker.

Form swords with both hands. Direct your right sword at your enemy's heart while keeping your left as a defensive measure. Recite the Kuji in your mind and when you get to Zen, focus on piercing your opponent's heart to stop him.

Haya Kuji 早九字
Rapid Nine Seals

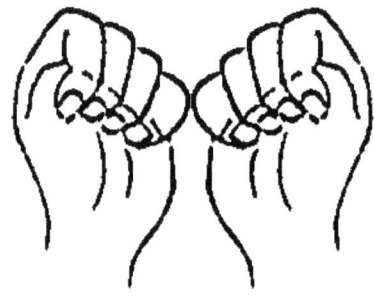

勝勝勝

Chant *Sho, Sho, Sho*, meaning victory, victory, victory while gripping your thumbs inside your fists. This is also known as Haya Kuji.[40]

The single Kanji Zen can represent all of the Kuji. This is what is being represented.

---

[40] In *Mikko* 密教 esoteric Buddhism, each finger represents one of the Five Agents.

Ko Yubi	小指 little finger	地 Earth
Kusuri Yubi	薬指 ring finger	水 Water
Naka Yubi	中指 Middle Finger	火 Fire
Hitosashi Yubi	人差し指 Index Finger	風 Wind
Oya Yubi	親指 Thumb	空 Void

右前ノ字ハ。一字ニテ上ノ八一字ノ意ヲ具フ。即九畫ナルベシ。嬶ノ字モ然。一字ニテ下ハ一字ノ意ヲ括ル。一畫ヲ一字ニテ中テ。九畫ニテ九字ノ意ヲ括ル。一畫ヲ一字ニテ中テ。八方ヲ兼ル。九畫ナリ。前字ハ中央ヲ主テ。八方ヲ兼ルニ中ル。八太陽ノ數摩利支天實瓶ノ仰ニ中ル。一字ニテ足ルコヲ知ルベシ。清浄之早九字ト云之ヲ精進。常ニ九字ヲ修行スルニ。熟スベシ。平生事ニ當テ。信心ニシテ眼前ニ有ノ如ク十ルベシ。日ニ修行懈ラズシテ。三十年ニ及ブ時ハ其驗アラム

Ichiji no Kuji 一字九字
One Kanji Nine Seals

Using just the Kanji Zen 前, Before, is called One Kanji Nine Seals. It relies on *Kannen* 観念 total focus and belief on the part of the user.

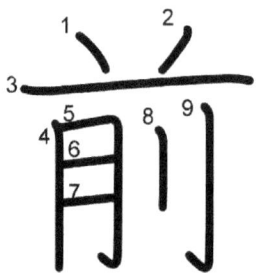

The single Kanji Zen, Before, contains the meaning of the preceding eight Kanji that make up the Kuji. It is a way of instantly writing all of the Kuji at once. The reason the Kanji Zen can be used this way is because it takes nine strokes to write it, which reflects the entirely of the Kuji.

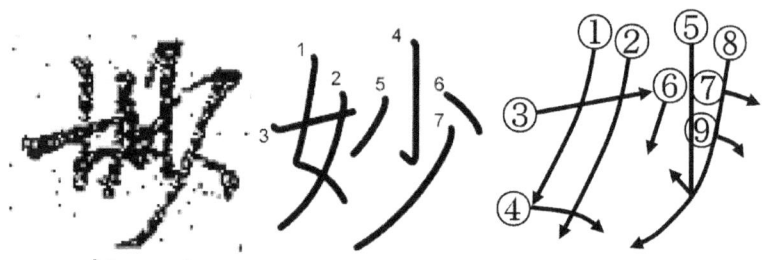

Left: The Kanji Myo with nine strokes from the text.
Center: The standard way to write Myo
Right: Order of the nine cuts to draw the Kanji Myo.

This is similar to how the Kanji Myo 妙 mysterious, was altered to have nine strokes. The meaning of the eight previous Kanji are entwined in a single Kanji.[41] Each stroke represents one Kanji.

---

[41] The Kuji, Nine Seals, used with the Kanji Myo, mysterious, are *Myoho-renge-kyo Johon Dai Ichi Kuji* 妙法蓮華経序品第一
The Number One Kuji of the Mysterious Lotus Sutra.

・井田之折形之事

```
┌─────┬─────┬─────┐
│ 鬪  │ 兵  │ 齕  │
├─────┼─────┼─────┤
│ 者  │ 前  │ 在  │
├─────┼─────┼─────┤
│ 皆  │ 陣  │ 列  │
└─────┴─────┴─────┘
```

白キ紙ヲ方ニメ圖ノ如ク折ル。鋏ヲ以テ圖ニ
如ク折ルベカラズ。按ズルニ
紙ヲ切ルベカラズシテ引サ
物ヲ不用シテ引サ
切ルヘ十字ニ折テ
キ四角ニスベシ其
方紙ヲ圖ノ如ク
圖ニ折形ヲ十
筆或ハ小刀ヲ以
二字ヲ書ス
テ九字ヲ書ス

Shojin Seijo no Haya Kuji 精進清浄之早九字
Dedicated Purifying Fast Nine Seals.

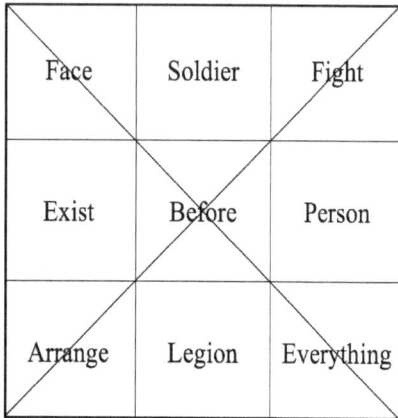

Rin 臨	Pyo 兵	To 闘
Zai 在	Zen 前	Sha 者
Retsu 列	Jin 陣	Kai 皆

Face	Soldier	Fight
Exist	Before	Person
Arrange	Legion	Everything

Marishiten Hobin no In 摩利支天寶瓶の印
Treasured Vase Seal of Marishiten, God of Rays of Light

Write the Kanji Zen in the center and arrange the other eight Kanji around it. Since the Kanji has nine strokes it represents Great Yang, and the Treasured Vase of Marishiten seal is used. Understand that this single Kanji is all that is required. This is called *Shojin Seijo no Haya Kuji* Dedicated Purifying Fast Nine Seals.

As you train Kuji you should be full of faith in the Three Treasures 三宝 which are the Buddha, the Dharma (the teachings of Buddha) and the Sangha (the community of monks and nuns.) By doing so you will begin to naturally notice how things are meant to appear in the course of your daily life. If you continue to practice daily over the course of three years without fail, you will certainly experience this.

Seiden no Origata no Koto 井田之折形之事
How to fold paper to reflect the well-field system[42]

Rin 臨	Pyo 兵	To 闘	Face	Soldier	Fight
Zai 在	Zen 前	Sha 者	Exist	Before	Person
Retsu 列	Jin 陣	Kai 皆	Arrange	Legion	Everything

First fold a blank sheet of paper as indicated by the lines in the diagram. When trimming the piece of paper from a larger sheet, do not cut the paper with an iron blade.

When folding the diagonal cross on the paper, do not use a knife. Next, fold the paper so that you end up with nine squares as shown in the illustration.[43] Finally, use a brush or small knife to draw each of the nine Kuji in a square on the sheet of paper.

---

[42] The well-field system was a Chinese land allocation method used between around 900~240 BC. Eight households each had a field to farm with a ninth field in the center. The crops produced by the communal field, which was maintained by all eight families, went to the government for famine distribution or to the king as tribute. The layout resembles the Kanji for well 井.

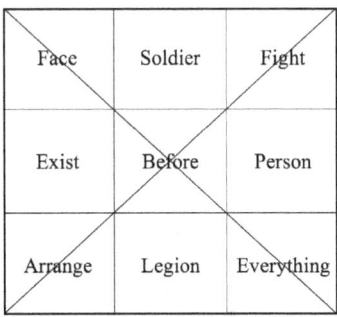

Private Farm	Private Farm	Private Farm
Private Farm	Communal Farm	Private Farm
Private Farm	Private Farm	Private Farm

[43] *Orikata* 折形 *describes traditional methods of folding letters inside paper envelopes. Some of the traditions in Samurai households are six hundred years old and describe how to properly fold letters and envelopes for various situations.*

-Yamane Orikata Manner Instruction Studio 山根折形礼法教室

一、血ノ縛リニハ。其疣上ニ當ルナリ無シ
一、穴ヲ塞ニ。是ヲ當レバ水モル丶コト無シ
一、歯血ウヅキニハ。其痛方ニ當レバ再ビ通ル丶コト無シ
一、鳥獣ノ通ル道ヲ塞バ。方ニ子シ
一、舟底ニ敷テ舟カヘル丶コトナシ
一、枕下ニ敷テ寢ル時ハ。守護トナル字利益多シ
一、此外其用ニ從テ用ベシ。
一、速ニ此法ヲ用ユルニハ。前字一字中央ニ書スベシ。故ニ
一、然ニ此法ハ。八門ノ九ノ星ニ中ルニ
一、九宮八門ノ法トモ云ヒ
一、叉物ヲ用ユル時ハ。木土水火金ト三遍
一、兄メ紙ヲ方ニ切ベシ

Applications of *Seiden no Origata no Koto* 井田之折形之事
Folded Paper Reflecting the Well-Field System

(1) This works as a Chi Shibari 血縛, an agent to stop a wound from bleeding.
(2) If you use this paper to plug a leak, water will not seep out.
(3) If your tooth is broken or bleeding, applying it to the spot will eliminate the pain.
(4) If you affix this to a trail that wild animals and birds use to cause you trouble, it will prevent them from passing again.
(5) If you put it on the bottom of a boat, the boat will never capsize.
(6) When you sleep with it under your pillow, it will protect you. There are many other situations where this can be applied. It will bring great benefit.
(7) To use the fast version of this spell, draw the Kanji Zen in the center. This spell is based on the Eight Gates and the Nine Stars. Thus it is referred to as the Eight Gates and Nine Palaces.[44]
(8) When using a knife, chant the following spell three times

「木土、水火金」

Wood and earth
Water, fire and metal

and then cut the paper along the lines.

---

[44] See the Translator's Note on the following pages.

Translator's Note: *Kimon Tonkotsu* 奇門遁甲

This refers to *Kimon Tonkotsu* 奇門遁甲 also known as Qimen Dunjia, a type of ancient divination for determining whether good or evil lies in a certain direction and how present or future events will transpire.

In about 3000 BC in China, the Lo River flooded. To calm the river God, they offered sacrifices. Suddenly, a big turtle emerged from the river, with a curious pattern on its shell: A magic square with a 3 × 3 grid, in which circular dots of numbers were arranged, such that the sum of the numbers in each row, column and diagonal was the same: Fifteen. Also any two numbers with five in the center add up to ten.

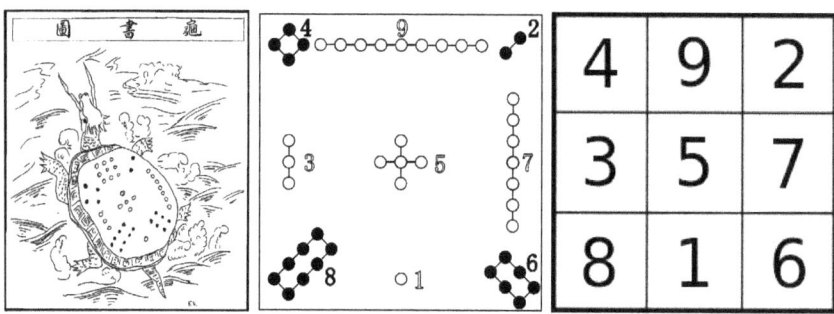

Thus, the Qimen Dunjia cosmic board consists of a 3 × 3 magic square of Nine Palaces 九宮 which represent all the directions of the compass and the center 門. The nine palaces are also known as the 九星, Nine Stars. The Nine Stars/ Palaces are:

一白 One White・二黒 Two Black 三碧 Three Blue
四緑 Four Green・五黄 Five Yellow・六白 Six White
七赤 Seven Red・八白 Eight White・九紫 Nine Purple.

As the illustration in the center shows, even numbers represent Earth/Yin and are black. The odd numbers represent Heaven/Yang and are white.

The Nine Stars/Palaces interreact with eight gates in this system. The Eight Gates are：

Open Gate 開門 ・ Rest Gate 休門 ・ Life Gate 生門
Harm Gate 傷門 ・ Delusion Gate 杜門 ・ Scenery Gate 景門
Fear Gate 驚門 ・ Death Gate 死門

Qimen Dunjia can be thought of as "Eight Gates Hiding Jia (the emperor)"

The system uses the Five Agents, Ten Stems, Twelve Branches, Eight Gates, Eight Gods, Nine Stars/ Palaces, Eight Trigrams, Ying and Yang, Travelling Horse, Emptiness, and a few other special combinations to generate a Qimen Chart to indicate the current and future events.

-Dougles Chan Qimen Academy

卍字之大事

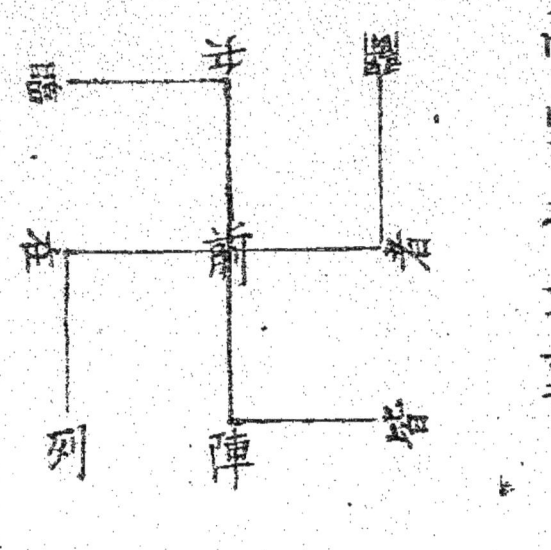

卍字ハ一畫ヅヽ点也。点スベシ。卍ニコノ如ク点ス也。
圖ノ臨点ヨリ先ス。
ベキ也。廾田ノ折形
ト意モ同ジ。故ニ用法
モ亦同ジ十ニリ起元
八門ノ九星ニシテ。
五行旺相死囚休ノ
二十五ニ中ル精ク
八九字秘解ニ具フ

SECRETS OF THE KUJI・九字秘傳

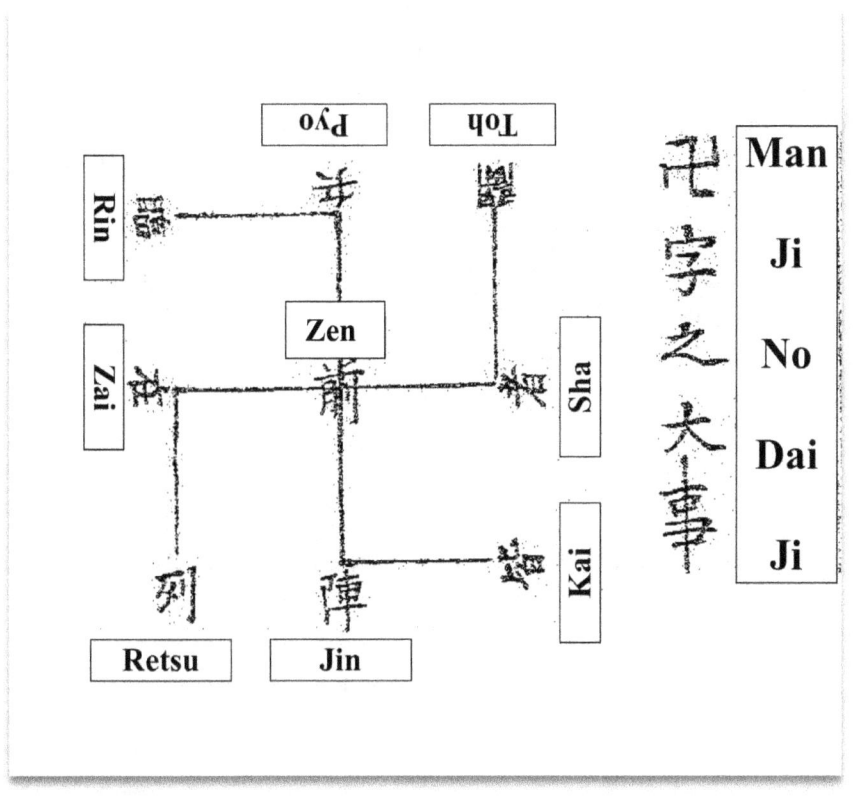

Manji no Daiji 卍字之大事
An Important Lesson About the Kanji Manji

The Kanji Manji, which stands for the Buddha,[45] is typically drawn with six strokes as follows:

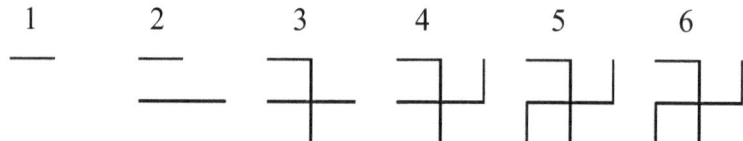

However for this spell, the Kanji should be drawn with nine strokes, one for each of the Kuji. You should begin with Rin. The meaning of this spell is the same as the Folded Paper Well-Field System spell. Thus these spells can be thought of as being the same.

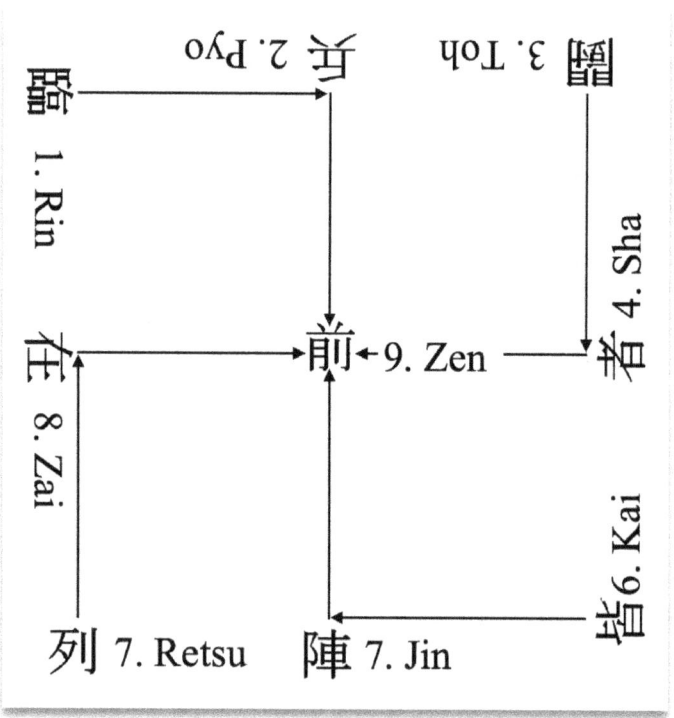

---

[45] 卍 is also used to indicate Buddhist temples on maps. Several Samurai families also used it as a family crest.

The spell has its origins in the Eight Gates and the Nine Stars. It also interacts with the five states:[46]

Ou 旺 Flourishing
So 相 Meeting
Shi 死 Dying
Shu 囚 Captured
Kyu 休 Resting

There are twenty five possible combinations. The exact meaning can be found in *Kuji Hikai* 九字秘解 Secrets of Kuji Explained[47]

---

[46] These five intervals of time reflect the changes in the seasons and are based on the Five Agents: Fire, Wood, Water, Earth, Air. *Ou* 旺 Flourishing, is the most vigorous while *Shi* 死 Dying, is the least.

[47] This appears to be another book about the Kuji by the same author.

元弓四方結之大事

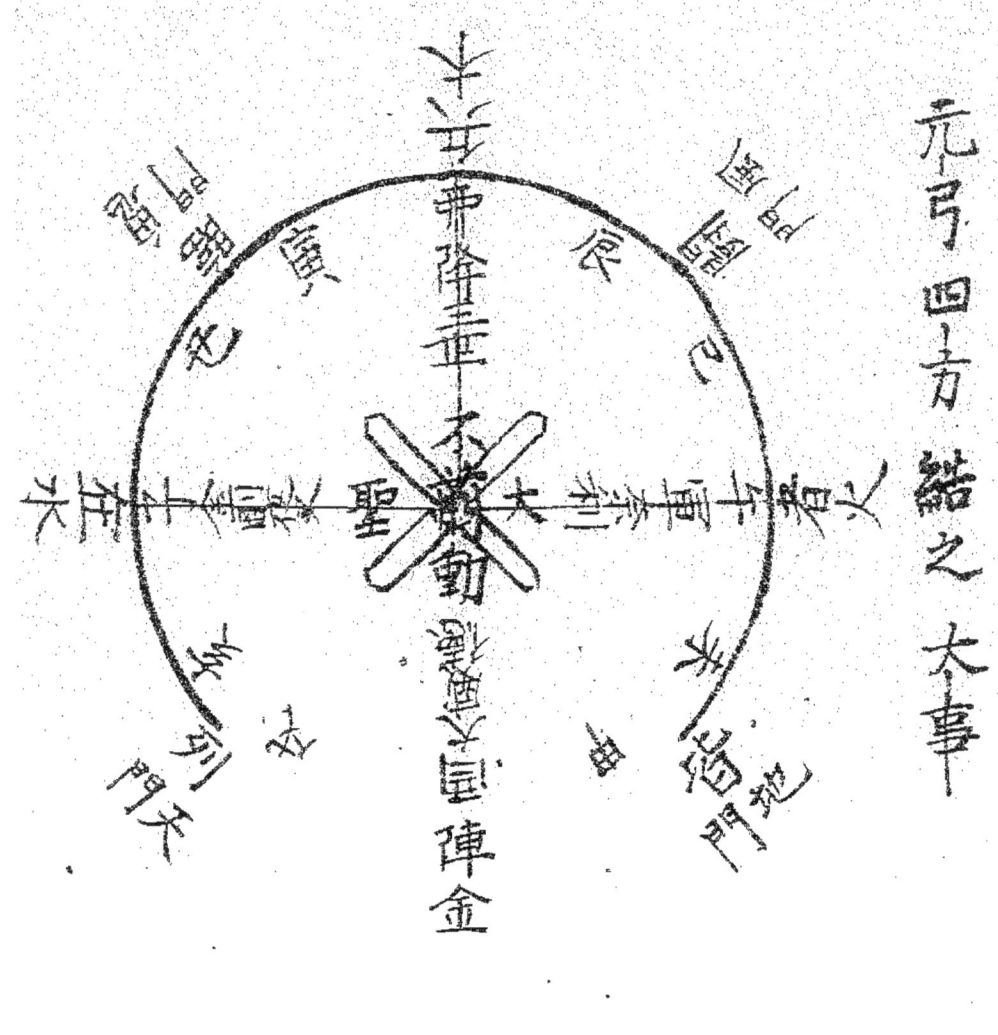

四方ノ結ニテ降伏ニ用ルナリ。
四大中央之不動主トシ
四明王ヲ主。
四方ヲ四門八門ニ合維ナリ。
維ト方也。
テ八方也。
加ニ中央ヲ九ナリ

Moto Yumi Shiho Tsuke no Daiji 元弓四方結之大事
Regarding the Original Bow Tied in Four Directions

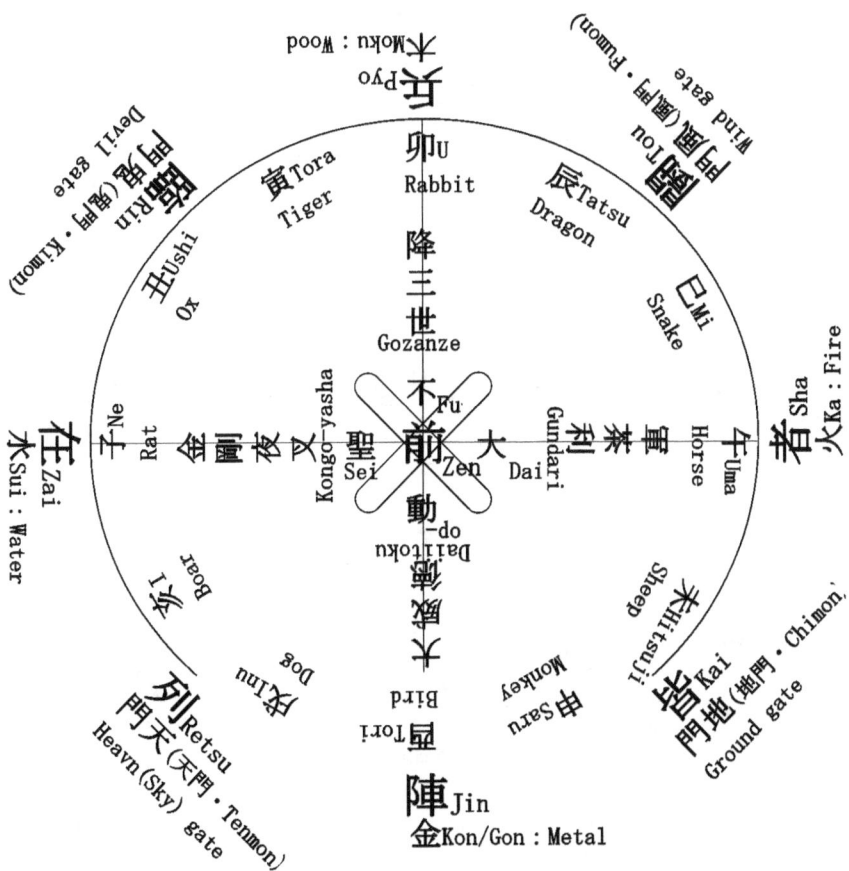

Moto Yumi Shiho Tsuke no Daiji 元弓四方結之大事
Regarding the Original Bow Tied in Four Directions

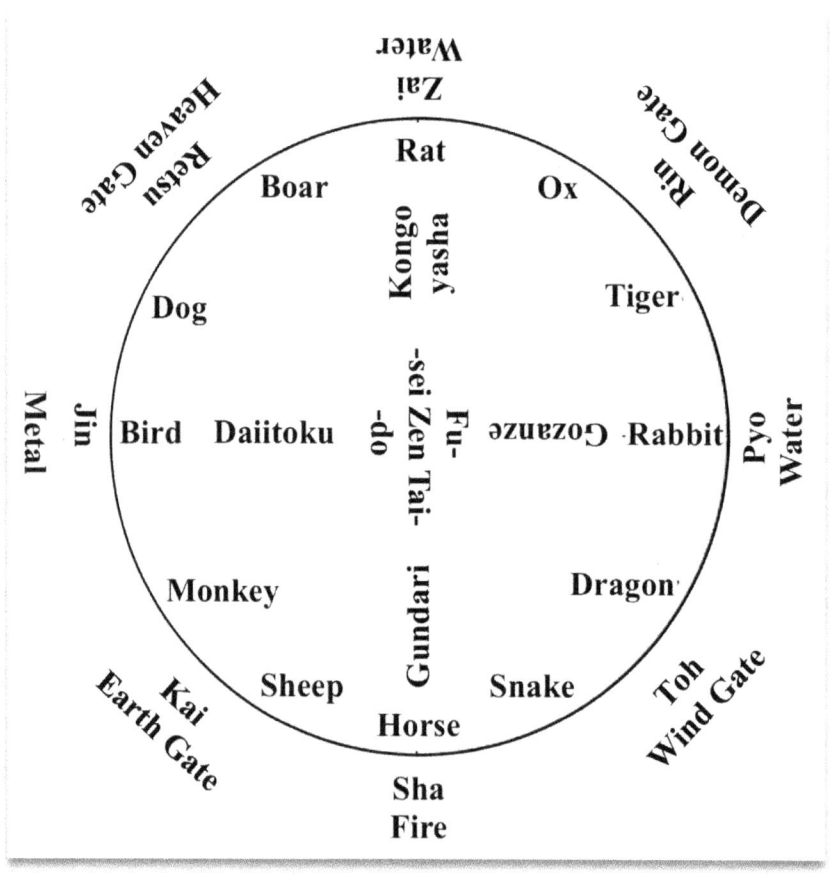

Moto Yumi Shiho Tsuke no Daiji 元弓四方結之大事
Regarding the Original Bow Tied in Four Directions[48]

The Four Direction tie is used to subdue any force acting against you, human or supernatural.[49] Fudo Myo-O, the Lord of Light Wisdom King, is in the center and the Four Great Lords of Light[50] are at each cardinal point. The Four Great Lords of Light command each of the four cardinal directions and the Four Gates control the ordinal directions. Combining these makes eight directions. Adding a center point makes nine.[51]

---

[48] *Moto Yumi* 元弓 Original Bo. This is another way to say *Meigen*, 鳴弦 plucking the bowstring to make a sound.
Shiho Musubi 四方結 The author does not define what this means but it likely refers to sweeping away evil in all directions proceeding clockwise from *Kimon* 鬼門 Devil's Gate or northeast. According to *An Introduction to the Secrets of Shingon Buddhism* 真言密教入門 You are dedicating yourself to *Gundari Myo-o* 軍荼利明王 Gundari Wisdom King. By chanting On-Sarasara-Basara-Hatsurakara-Unpatsuda the seal will surround you with a fence that is iron strong and will obliterate any evil.

[49] Gobuku 降伏 This implies using supernatural power to obliterate either evil spirits or anything troubling you including the hatred of enemies that has been directed at you. In Shingon Mikkyo a person who has learned this art can utilize the power of the Buddha to vanquish evil and demons. It is known as *Kofuku Ho* 降伏法 Submission Method or *Chobuku* Ho 調伏法 Exorcism.

[50] *Yondai* 四大 The four wisdom Kings (see Translator's Note on the following page.

[51] *Shi-i* 四維 four ordinal directions.

Translator's Note: The Four Wisdom Kings
The four wisdom Kings actually refers to the five wisdom kings Kongoyasha, Daiitoku, Gozanze and Gundari arranged with Taisei at the center controlling.

Tenmon Heaven Gate	Kongoyasha	Kimon Devil Gate
Daiitoku	Taisei	Gozanze
Chimon Earth Gate	Gundari	Fumon Wind Gate

枕加持之大事

臨兵闘者皆陣列在前 ䷀
　　　　　　　　　四ハ竪
　　　　　　　　　五ハ横

右枕ノ下ニ敷ナリ。寐ルトキ四竪五
横ニ切レ之ヲ
義経ノ枕加持ノ大事ト云ハ是ナリ
真言比丘ヨリ相傳スル所ナリ

臭氣ヲ留塞大事
是ハ不浄ノ氣ノ塞グ法ナリ。其法先
ヅ水ヲ満テ。水ノ面ニ筆又ハ小刀或

Makura no Kaji Daiji 枕之加持大事
An Important Lesson: Placing a Prayer Under Your Pillow[52]

Rin	Pyo	Toh	Sha	Kai	Jin	Retsu	Zai	井	Zen
臨	兵	闘	者	皆	陣	列	在		前

Face, Soldier, Fight, Person, Everything, Legion, Arrange, Exist, Before
When facing a powerful force of soldiers, those that seek to fight all break ranks and move to the vanguard.

Place the spell described above under your pillow. Just before you go to bed, cut the Four Vertical and Five Horizontal Lines.[53] This is Yoshitsune's[54] Placing a Prayer Under Your Pillow. It was handed down by an ordained Shingon priest.

---

[52] Kaji 加持 an incantation to rid yourself of misfortune or disease by receiving the blessing of the Buddha.
[53] The positioning of the Four Vertical and Five Horizontal Lines drawing before Zen, seems to imply that is the first eight Kanji are chanted, the 4x5 grid is drawn and then Zen is chanted.
[54] Referring to Minamoto no Yoshitsune 源義経 (1159 ~1189.)

Shu-e wo Rusai Daiji 臭穢を留塞大事
An Important Lesson: Keeping Foul, Unclean Smells Away

This is a method for walling yourself off from unclean spirit. Fill a vessel up to the top with water and use a brush or knife to draw the following Kanji on the surface of the water. You can also draw them with the Nito-in, Two-Sword Seal.

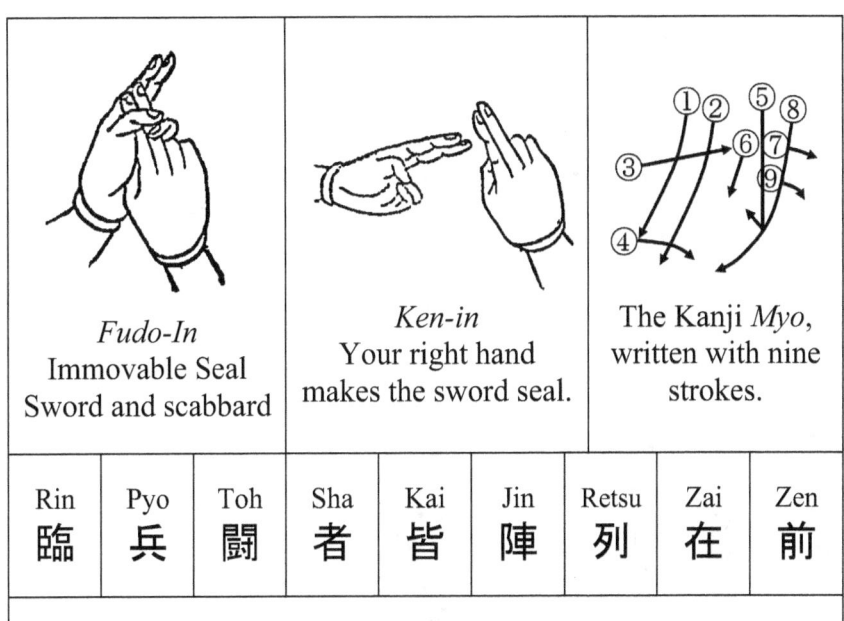

Fudo-In Immovable Seal Sword and scabbard	*Ken-in* Your right hand makes the sword seal.	The Kanji *Myo*, written with nine strokes.

Rin	Pyo	Toh	Sha	Kai	Jin	Retsu	Zai	Zen
臨	兵	闘	者	皆	陣	列	在	前

Face, Soldier, Fight, Person, Everything, Legion, Arrange, Exist, Before
When facing a powerful force of soldiers, those that seek to fight all break ranks and move to the vanguard.

If you follow the previously described procedures, then the odor of feces or other bad smells will not affect you.

You can also use this same spell to stop bleeding by drawing the Kanji Myo directly on top of the wound.

ハ劍卯之ニ仰ニテ畫レ之ヲ

妙臨兵鬪者皆陣列在前

右ノ如クスレバ畫臭ナド内ヘ不ハ入
一血ヲ止ニ。疣上ニ畫ス之右ノ如ク可シ畫ス

血縛ノ大變
是ハ疣ヲ員タル二。疣上ニ筆或ハ小
刀又ハ二刀卯ニテ畫レ之ヲ

妙大實
妙字ヲ九字ニ申ルナリ

SECRETS OF THE KUJI・九字秘傳

Ketsu Shibari no Daiji 血縛の大事
How to Stop Bleeding

You can stop a wound from bleeding by drawing these Kanji on top of the wound. Use a brush, a small knife, or the *Nito-in* 二刀印, Two-Sword Seal.[55]

	Nito-in Two-Sword Seal
	Myo **mysterious**
大	***Dai*** **Great**
寶	***Ho*** **Treasure**

---

[55] This explanation is lacking many details but seems to say after you draw your Ken-in, sword seal from your left hand (representing the scabbard) your left hand also serves as a sword. Other Kuji books indicate you use the middle finger to actually draw the Kanji.

・咽喉剌箋ヲ拔事
是ハ喉ニタチタル魚骨或ハ何ニテ
モ拔取法ナリ

娍是空
字共ニ九ノ畫九ノ字ニ中ル。
字中左右ト三ノ行ニ書ハ共ニ九ノ
字ナリ。盃中ノ類器ノ中ニ筆
ヲ以テ書シ、以レ墨ヲコレヲ塗盡
テ、他見ヲ不レ許ナリ。水ニテ
解テ吞ベシ

・如是空　則是空　卽是空。以上三ツ
呂共ニ同支ナリ。妙字ハ九字ニ不レ中
トモ。是空ノニ字テテ亙。赤空字ニ心

Inko Shisen wo Nuku Koto 咽喉刺簽を拔事
Removing a Stick Caught in Your Throat

This is a method for removing a fishbone or any other object from your throat. The three Kanji shown are all written with nine strokes.[56]

Myo Mysterious

Ze Justice

Ku Sky or Void

---

[56] The Kanji 是 is already written with nine strokes however the standard way of writing the other two Kanji has been adjusted. In the case of 妙 two extra strokes are added. In the case of 空 the third stroke has been divided into two separate strokes.

By writing three rows of these three Kanji you end up with nine Kanji, or Kuji.

You should write these Kanji on the inside of a dish used to drink Sake. After writing them paint over them with ink so that so that the characters cannot be seen by anyone else. Then dissolve the ink in water and drink it.

SECRETS OF THE KUJI・九字秘傳

如	Ultimate Nature	則	Rules	即	Instant
是	Justice	是	Justice	是	Justice
空	Void	空	Void	空	Void

In addition, the above three sequences of three Kanji can be used in the same as the previous technique. They are known as *San-ke* 三禼, the Three Slakenings of the Mouth.[57] While the Kanji 如 is not drawn with nine strokes, it is not considered to be part of the Kuji. However the following two Kanji Justice 是 and Void 空 do contain nine strokes to make up for this.

---

[57] *Kei* 禼 is a variation of the Kanji 和 and in this case refers to your mouth slackening. The "three slakenings" can possibly refer to how the mouth can be the source of disaster.

In addition, the Kanji Justice, can be used on its own if you do not wish to utilize the Kanji Ku, Void, and its underlying principles. The Kanji Justice is composed of three elements :

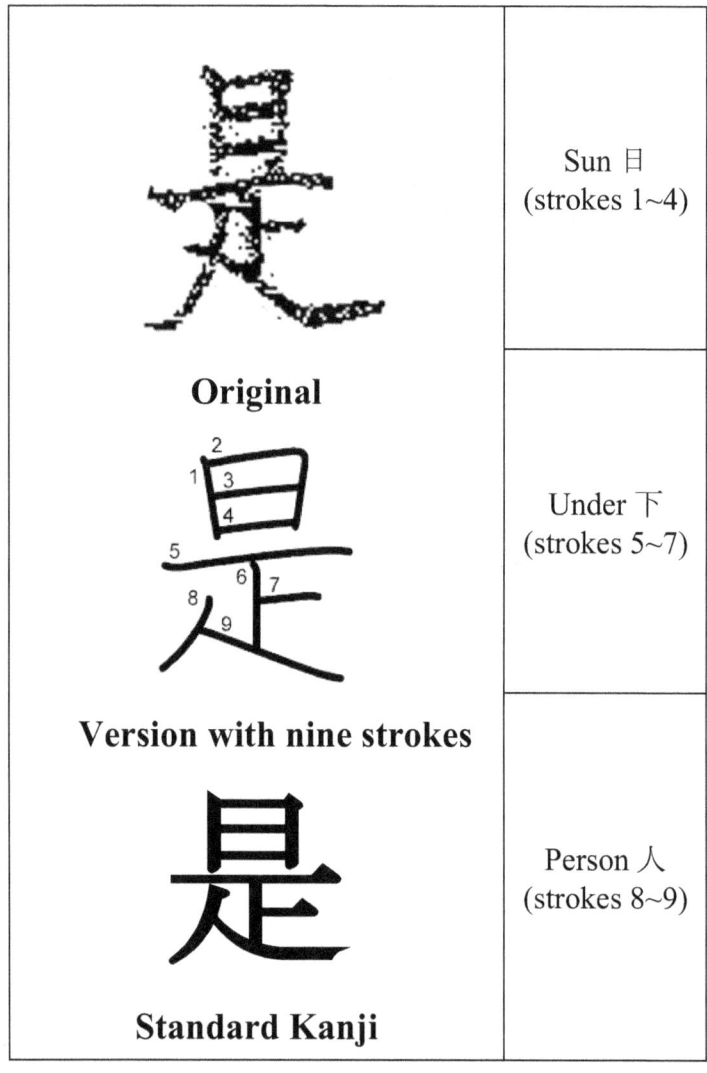

Sun 日, under 下, person 人 and should be written with the meaning of "a person under the sun." A "person under the sun 日下人" refers to "a person under heaven 天下人" or a man that has completely unified a country.

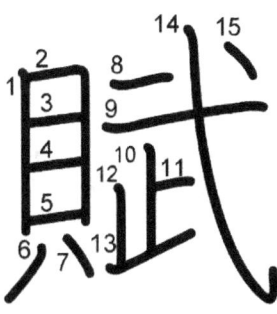

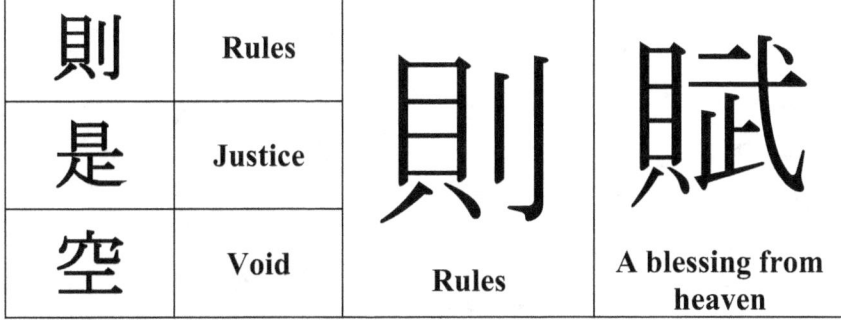

The Kanji 則 Rules, should be thought of a meaning *Nihonto*, a Japanese sword. This is similar to what the Kanji *Fu* 賦 a blessing from heaven, represents. The Kanji Fu also serves to represent the 12th emperor of Japan Yamato Takeru (72~112AD) so these concepts should be considered the same.

一、喉ニ夕ヲ開サセ書ニ直ニ切ヲ開サセテ小刀ニテ鵜ノ字ヲ三字書。其人ノ口ヲ開サセテ小刀ニテ鵜ノ字ヲ三字書。其人ノ口切べキ也。其鵜ノ字直ニ切レ也。其佗咄ト云ハシムレバ其骨ヲドリ出ルナリ

則字ハ日本人ト意得テ書ベシ。日本武ト意得ド同吏ナリ。日本刀ト意得べシ。コレ賦字ナリ。是字ヲ日下人ト意得テ書べシ。ヲッケズメモ。是字バカリニテ不若

如レ是品ノ中ニ筆メ。墨ニテ塗リ。水ニ觧。吞モ宜

[囲み: 八音神護身]

Removing a Bone Caught in Your Throat

Rai
Dusty thrush

This method can also use this to remove a fish bone lodged in a person's throat. First, open the person's mouth, and use a small knife to write the Kanji *Rai* 鶇 which refers to the dusky thrush or any bird that resembles it. What I mean by this is you should draw the Kanji in the air in front of the person afflicted three times.

Next, immediately chant the Kuji while cutting the Four Vertical and Five Horizontal Lines. You can also use the same small knife you used to draw the Kanji *Rai* to cut the Four Vertical and Five Horizontal Lines as you chant the Kuji. Then, use a small knife for cutting paper, to slice the Kanji *Rai* you drew in the air. If you click your tongue while doing this the bone will fly out.

Removing a Stick Caught in Your Throat: Version 2

Another way to do this method is to draw the following talisman on the inside of a dish. Cover the drawing with ink and then fill the vessel with water and drink it down.

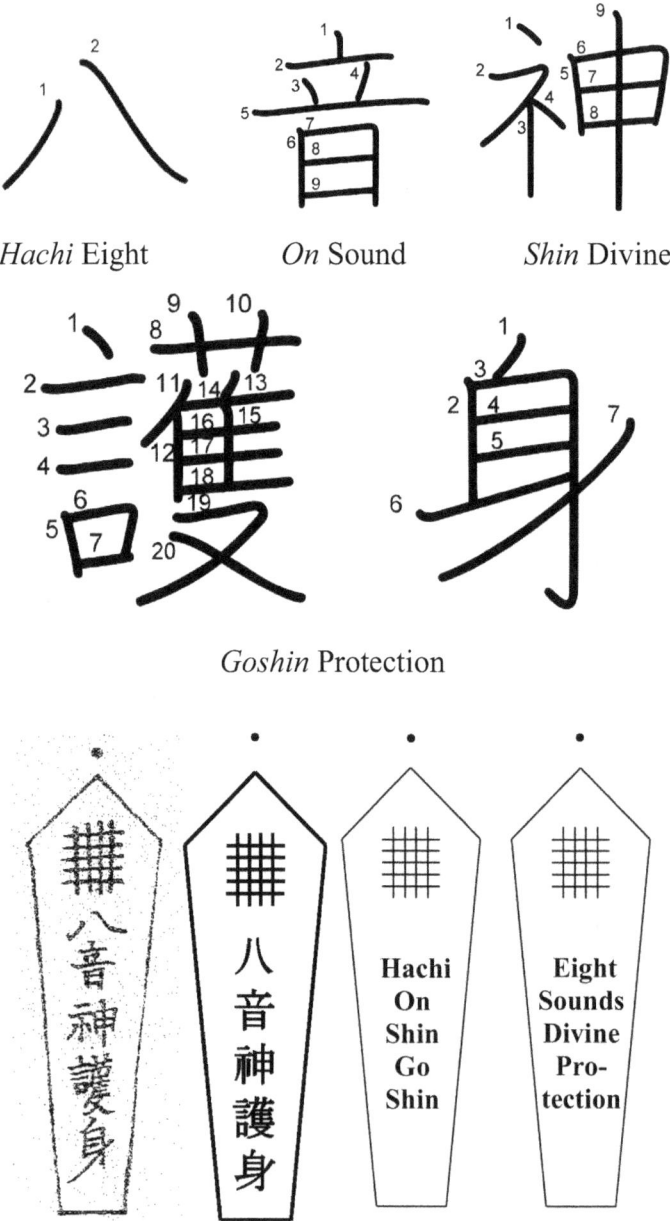

Hachi Eight *On* Sound *Shin* Divine

Goshin Protection

右四ノ竪五ノ横ハ則九ノ龍タルニ依リテ
九龍ハ音神護身ト直ニ書モ同此
符ハ骨ニ不レ限咽ノ刺篏ニ用ベシ

虎

・在犬ヲ縛ル事

九畫九字ニ中ル十リ。二刀卯ニ
テ其犬ニ向テ一心ニ畫ス其卯
ヲ強クシムルナリ。卯ヲ解ハ其
縛解ルナリ

・鞘縛リノ大事

先 不動卯 臨兵閥者皆陣列在前

Kyu Ryu 九龍
Nine Dragons

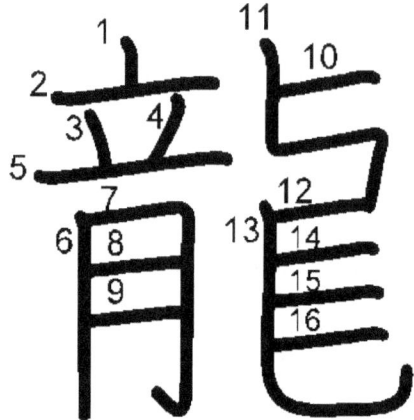

The Kanji *Ryu* 龍 dragon, can also be used with the previous method of drawing the Four Vertical and Five Horizontal Lines within a sword shaped talisman.

This method is called *Kyuryu Hachion Shin Goshin* 九龍八音神護身 Nine Dragons Eight Sounds Divine Protection.[58] Once you make this talisman, it is not just effective on bones stuck in your throat, but anything stuck in your throat.

---

[58] "Nine Dragons" refers to chanting the Kuji as you draw the Four Vertical and Five Horizontal Lines. The *Hachi-On*, Eight Voices, describe the eight ways of speaking used in Buddhist sermons. The eight voices were first described in *The Essentials of Rebirth in the Pure Land* 往生要集 which was an influential medieval Buddhist text composed in 985 by the monk Genshin.

Kyokko	極好	Superior Voice
Nyunan	柔輭	A soft voice (Soft as a result of becoming enlightened to the teachings of the Buddha.)
Wachaku	和適	The perfect volume
Sone	慧	Majestic voice
Fujo	不女	Cheerful and melodious
Fugo	不誤	A voice that makes no errors with words
Shin-non	深遠	A resonant voice that carries far
Fukatsu	不竭	A clear, easy to understand voice

Kyoken wo Shibaru Koto 狂犬を縛る事
How to Restrain a Mad Dog

Standard Tiger   Book Version   Stroke Order

The Kanji *Tora*, tiger, is typically drawn as shown on the left. For this talisman it has been altered so that it is drawn with nine strokes, as shown on the right.

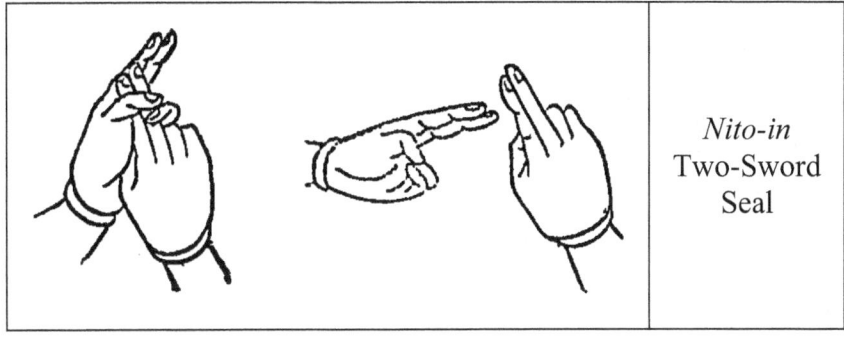

Nito-in Two-Sword Seal

Since Tiger is written with nine strokes it represents all the Kuji. Form the *Nito-in*, two-sword seal, and point it at the dog.[59] Focus your mind completely and draw this Kanji. This will bind the animal tightly. If you release the seal, the bond holding the dog will also release.

---

[59] The author refers to the Two Sword Seal as *Ken-in* and *Toh-in*, however they refer to the same thing.

Saya Shibari no Daiji 鞘縛りの大事
How to Lock Your Opponent's Sword in His Sheath

This technique begins by chanting the Kanji *Saki* 先, meaning First. This is because you must focus all your spirit into the previously described Fudo-in, Immovable Seal, in order to form this seal powerfully. Then chant,

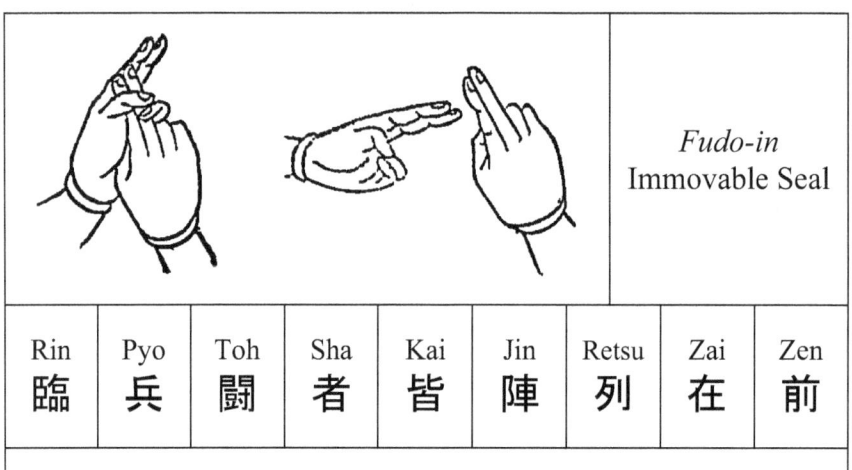

								Fudo-in Immovable Seal
Rin 臨	Pyo 兵	Toh 闘	Sha 者	Kai 皆	Jin 陣	Retsu 列	Zai 在	Zen 前

Face, Soldier, Fight, Person, Everything, Legion, Arrange, Exist, Before

When facing a powerful force of soldiers, those that seek to fight all break ranks and move to the vanguard.

You must make this seal powerfully. If you pour all your faith into your Kuji spell, your opponent will be rendered unable to draw his sword from his sheath.

右卯ヲ強クシムルナリ。而ノ九ノ字ヲ
念誦スベシ。敵又ヲ抜ヿアタハズ
・前邊ノ法ノ裏

上畧　暈鎧品軍　唵急如律令 ※

中畧　暈法品軍　唵急如律令 ☰

下畧　舍屍蕆砰軍不　唵急如律令 ☰

右ハ黃石公ノ三ノ畧ノ法ト云傳フ

Yachigai no Ho 箭違の法の事
Talismans to make your oppoennt choose the wrong arrow
Joryaku 上畧 **Upper Strategy**

暈鋥品軍唸急如律令 ䷀☆☆

This talisman consists of three parts. First write,

> Halo-Metal Derived-Goods-Army[60]

Followed by,

> *Kyu-Kyu-Nyo-Ritsu-Ryo*
> *Immediately execute my orders according to the ancient law.*
> *(Please immediately grant my wish.)*[61]

Finally draw the Four Horizontal and Five Vertical Lines.[62]

---

[60] The second Kanji 鋥 is of unknown meaning. It was probably created as a kind of spell within itself and contains unknown attributes and powers. Since the left side has the element "metal 金" the name Metal-Derived is used.

[61] *Ritsuryo* were the criminal, administrative and civil codes that began in Han Era China (202 BC ~220 AD) which were also used in Japan in the Nara and Heian eras (710~1185 AD.) The phrase *Immediately execute my orders according to the ancient law* was added to the end of official documents indicating the receiver should immediately act on the orders received. In Japan *Onmyoji*, court sorcerers, and *Kitoshi*, official fortune tellers, added this phrase to the end of their spells as a way to banish evil spirits. For the layman the phrase was probably interpreted as *Please immediately grant my wish.*

[62] The book does not mention this but the Four Horizontal and Five Vertical Lines combined with a pentagram are associated with the court sorcerers Abe no Seimei 安倍晴明 (921 ~ 1005) and Ashiya Doman 蘆屋道満 (12th century AD.) These two symbols together can be referred to as Seiman (the star)-Doman (horizontal/vertical lines.)

Churyaku 中畧 Center Strategy

暈法嘂軍　唸急如律令 𠃌

This talisman consists of three parts. First write,

> Halo-Method-Essential[63]-Army,

Followed by,

> Kyu-Kyu-Nyo-Ritsu-Ryo
> Immediately execute my orders according to the ancient law.

Finally, draw the Four Horizontal and Five Vertical Lines.

---

[63] 嘂 要

The Kanji 嘂 is an alternate way to write the Kanji 要 which can mean Essential, Fundamental or Keystone.

Lower Strategy 下署

舍屍競䇞軍㊅ 唵急如律令卌

This talisman consists of three parts. First write,

A Day's March-Butt-Dragon-Hand Guard of Your Sword,[64]

Next, draw the Kanji 不 inside the shape as shown.

After that, write,

Kyu-Kyu-Nyo-Ritsu-Ryo Rei
Immediately execute my orders according to the ancient law.

Finally, draw the Four Vertical and Five Horizontal Lines.

The above are called *Sanryaku no Ho*, 三略の法 the *Three Strategies* and are attributed to Huang Shigong 黃石公 Yellow Rock Old Man, a Taoist immortal.[65]

---

[64] The first Kanji 舍 or A Day's March refers to the prescribed marching distance of an army in ancient China 12.2 km/7.6 miles. There is no explanation of why the Kanji 不 which means "not" or "un-"(to negate something) is inside the small drawing.

[65] Generally speaking, these talismans would be written vertically with a brush on traditional Japanese paper.

一 上ノ署ハ髷ノウケ張ノ中ニ納ムベシ
一 中ノ署ハ上帶ニ納ムルナリ
一 下ノ署ハ呑ベキナリ
一 三ノ署ヲ一ツニ書テ具足ノ脇板ニ納ムベシ。此誓ノ的ニメ試ムルニ。矢反テ不中ト云ヘリ
一 書法ハ其人ノ血ヲ取テ。朱ニ和メ。赤地ノ錦ニ可書ナリ
一 小兒ノ夜鳴ヲ止大事
・小兒ノ夜啼ニ。其元色々アリ。其兒ノ衣類或ハフクサモノ類失フベカ

After drawing the Upper Strategy talisman fold it up inside your *Ukebaru* 浮張, the folded cloth placed inside your helmet as padding.

After drawing the Middle Strategy talisman fold it up inside the *Uwaobi* 上帯, the final belt that goes over your armor and holds your swords in place.

After drawing the Lower Strategy talisman, swallow it.

If you draw the *Sanryaku*, all three spells, then place it under the breastplate of your armor. You can test this talisman by drawing it and attempting to shoot an arrow at it. It will always miss.

The way to draw this talisman is for the writer to take some of his own blood, mix it with some crimson ink and then draw it on a piece of cotton cloth that has been dyed red.

Shoji no Yonaki wo Tomeru Daiji 小児の夜鳴を止大事
An Important Lesson: How to stop a child from crying at night.

There are many different reasons a child might be crying at night. It is important to remember to keep track of your child's clothing, or silk blanket.[66]

Draw this talisman vertically on a piece of paper to stop a child from crying.

虎 ☆ ☆ 前 唵急如律令

The first Kanji is Tora, tiger, but drawn with nine strokes. Next are two pentagrams, the first slightly smaller than the second. After that draw the Kanji Zen, Before, and finally,
  Kyu-Kyu-Nyo-Ritsu-Ryo Rei
  Immediately execute my orders according to the ancient law.

---

[66] The blanket being described is a *Fukusa* 袱紗 a small cloth made of silk.

ラズ。狐狸ノ類得レ之ルトキハ。之ヲ其兒ノ腹ナドニ懸フ心ニテ。呪メナブリヘリサケルナリ。然ル時ハ必夜啼ヲビヘフナドスル者ナリ。人ナドニモ盗ラレナカレ。糞精ヲヌバヒタル紙類自ラ結ツカヒタル楊枝髮ヲヌワゲタル元結是等ヲ慎テ失フフナカルベシ。大人小兒共ニ同夫ナリ

虎☰☆前 唵急如律令

There is a reason it is important not to lose your child's clothing or blankets. If diabolical tricksters like foxes or raccoons come in contact with your child, they can gain control over them. This can happen if they smell your child's clothing or sometimes by sight alone. The creature can then take control of your child and manipulate them. When a child cries at night it may be because they sense the supernatural forces within their belly and are frightened of the creature exerting control over them.

This is the same as if someone steals the paper you use to wipe up your feces or semen,[67] toothpicks, or the piece of string you use to tie your topknot. It is essential that you exercise caution so that you do not to lose any of these things. This applies to both adults and children.

---

[67] There is another possible meaning for *Fun-Sei* 糞精 feces and semen and that is *Funkasu* 糞糟 "Excrement leavings" which refers to water extracted from a latrine. The process consists of,

Cutting a section of bamboo with the joints still intact on either end in the final month of the year. You then shave off the outer layer of the bamboo and submerge the section in the latrine. On the first day of the new year, remove the bamboo section from the latrine. It will be full of water that has permeated the void inside the bamboo, filtered by the bamboo.

The water inside has medicinal properties. So the Kanji 精 does not refer to sperm but to extracting the vital essence from feces. Making medicines from human excrement is also called *Jinchu-o* 人中黄 The Yellow from Inside Man.

-*Manshu Magazine* 満蒙 12(8)(136)
By Takeda Nanyo
August 1931

右虎ノ骨ヲ末メ朱ニ和シテ。此ノ如ク可調ナリ。上ノ包シテ。表ニ右ノ朱ヲ以テ。左ノ如ク書スナリ。

賦　前護身

著ノ如ク上ニ書ス。折カケ包ナリ。寢所ノ枕ノ上ノ柱ニ張ベシ。必夜ノ啼止也。

一、小兒ノ額ニ右ノ朱ニテ前字ヲ一字畫スレバ夜啼必止モノナリ。

瘧疾之厭勝ノ事

譬ハ五發ト云ハ。九ノ字ノ五ノ字メ。皆

Ink for the "stopping a child from crying at night" talisman

Draw this talisman vertically on a piece of paper to stop a child from crying.

虎☆☆ 前 噁急如律令

Make the ink by mixing powdered tiger bone and cinnabar. Next, write the talisman as shown above. Wrap this in a paper envelope and, using the above red ink mixture write the Kanji as shown below. Then fold the paper envelope up and paste it onto the side of your child's pillow. This will absolutely stop crying at night.

 賊	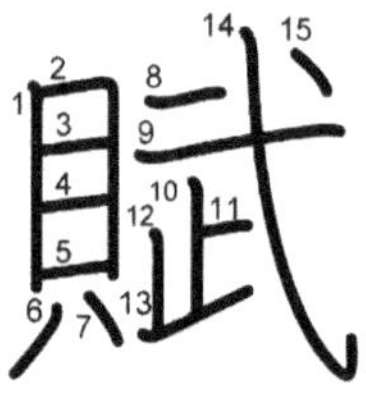 賊	賊 Thief
 前	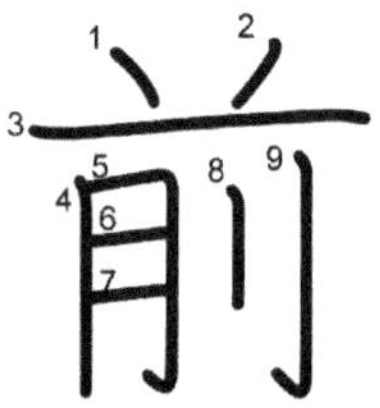 前	前 Before
 護身	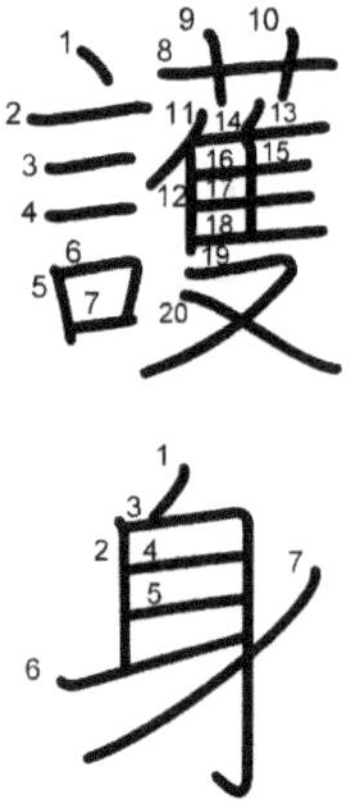 護身	護身 *Goshin* Self-Protection

Alternate Method

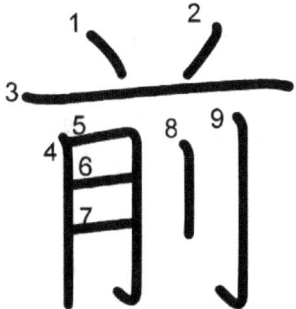

Using the aforementioned red ink, write the Kanji Zen 前 on the child's forehead. By writing the entirety of the Kuji using only one Kanji, it will absolutely stop a child from crying at night.

字ヲ用ヰ或ハ三ヲ發メナラバ闘字ヲ用。亦ハ十發メナド、云ハバ、十ノ内、九ヲ去テ余一。則一ノ臨字ヲ用。二ノ十發メナラバ九ヲ去テ余二。則兵字ヲ用

一二三四五六七八九十十一十二十三十四十五
兵闘者皆陣列在前

右其中ヲ用字ヲ。小方紙ニ書十リ井花水ノ朝始ニム水ヲ以テ。辰砂ヲ解キ龍骨ト虎骨トノ細末ヲ和テ。之ヲ以テ書ナリ。而メ之ヲ丸メ。其發旦ノ朝、井花水ニテ。日出ニ向テ呑ベシ。他ニ見ス

Gyakushitsu no Yosho no Koto 瘧疾之厭勝の事
How to Suppress a Sudden Fever[68]

For example if a patient is suffering from *Go Furui* 五發, the fifth outbreak of a fever or illness, you would treat it by using the fifth Kanji in the Kuji. In that case you would use the Kanji *Kai* 皆 everything and everyone.

Or if it is the *San Furui* 三發, third outbreak of a fever or illness, you would use the third Kanji, namely *To*h 鬪 Fight.

There is also a spell known as *Ju Furui* 十發 the tenth outbreak of fever or illness. For this you use the Kanji *Rin* 臨 to Face, since after going through all nine Kanji of the Kuji you return to the first.

Thus if you are dealing with the twentieth outbreak of a fever or illness then subtract 9 from 20 and then subtract 2 more. This will give you *Pyo* 兵 Soldier.

1	2	3	4	5	6	7	8	9
Rin 臨	Pyo 兵	Toh 鬪	Sha 者	Kai 皆	Jin 陣	Retsu 列	Zai 在	Zen 前
10	11	12	13	14	15	16	17	18
Rin 臨	Pyo 兵	Toh 鬪	Sha 者	Kai 皆	Jin 陣	Retsu 列	Zai 在	Zen 前
19	20	21	22	23	24	25	26	27

When using the Kanji described above, write them on a small square of paper. Make the calligraphy ink with *Seikasui* 井花水, "flower well water." This refers to water drawn from a well between the hours of the Ox and the Tiger (2:00 ~4:00 a.m.) [69]

---

[68] *Gyakushitsu* 瘧疾 describes a fever that comes on suddenly. But also describes an person who angers easily.
Assho 厭勝 another word for spell or curse.
[69] *Seikasui* 井花水 This water is considered the clearest and coolest and is used for medicines and when offerings water to the gods.

Take flower well water and use it to dissolve "dragon sand," or cinnabar. Next, take dragon bone[70] and tiger bone and powder them and add them to the mix.

Use this ink to draw the talisman with the appropriate Kuji based on the number of times the disease has manifest. Next, roll the paper talisman up into a ball. On the morning of the first day you come down with a fever, face the morning sun and drink the balled up talisman with flower well water.

This talisman should never be shown to others, thus the Kanji should be covered by the aforementioned cinnabar after you draw it.

---

[70] Dragon bones are the fossilized bones of any mammal.

一 發日ノ朝男ハ左。女ハ右。掌中ニ其中ニテ塗リ蓋フベシ。ルノヲ不レ許。故ニ文字ノ上ヲ。右ノ辰砂リ用ユ字ヲ。右ノ辰砂等ヲ以テ。井花水ニテ筆畫スレバ。必癰瘡治スル也。最モ文字上ヲ塗義前ノ如シ

虎 發日ノ朝用ベシ。必治スル也辰砂ヲ以テ。井花水ニテ。虎骨ノ末ヲ和シ。鳩ノ尾ニ畫メ字上ヲ塗。

一 右ノ辰砂虎骨ノ和ヲ以テ鳩ノ尾ニ四縱五ノ横ヲ用モ宜。赤虎字ノ時ハ龍骨辰砂ノ和ヲ用モ宜。何レモ發日ノ朝

Alternate Method 1

On the morning of the first day the disease presents itself, you should write the appropriate Kanji on your palm, based on how many times the fever or illness has manifest itself. Men should write it on their left palm, women on their right palm. For ink, use the previously mentioned dragon sand (cinnabar) along with flower well water, water taken from a well between the hours of 2~4 AM.

Using this spell will cause the sudden fever to dissipate quickly and you will recover. As before, it is important to paint over the Kanji after you draw it.

Alternate Method 2

Standard Tiger   Book Version   Stroke Order

Dissolve dragon sand (cinnabar) in flower well water and then add powdered tiger bone. Write the above Kanji, meaning tiger, on your solar plexus and then cover it. Use this spell on the morning of your illness. It will invariably heal you.

Alternate Method 3

Dissolve dragon sand (cinnabar) in flower well water and then add powdered tiger bone. Draw the Four Horizontal and Five Vertical Lines on your solar plexus and cover it. Use this spell on the morning of your illness. It will invariably heal you.

馬上芝繋之大事

人ノ馬ニ乗リ來ルヲ其ノ馬ヲ繋グモ
馬上ニテ吾乗タル馬ヲ繋グモ此ノ二ノ法
共ニ芝繋ト云

人ノ無キ馬ヲ繋グ法

不動印　臨兵闘者皆陣列在前
右印ヲ結テ馬ノ歩足ニ中元九字ヲ
念誦メ前ノ字ニテ印ヲ強クシムル也
急速ニハ靱縛ト同事

吾乗馬ヲ繋グ法

Bajo Shiba Tsunagi no Daiji 馬上芝繋之大事
**An Important Lesson:
How to Secure Your Horse When Mounted**

Shiba Tsunagi refers to securing your horse to a tree or to the ground. When you are ready to mount a horse this method is used to tie the horse in place. It can also be used when you are riding on a horse and wish to secure it in place. Both of these methods are known as *Shiba Tsunagi*, securing to the grass.

Hito no Joba wo Tsunagiho 人の乗馬を繋法
How to Secure a Horse While Riding

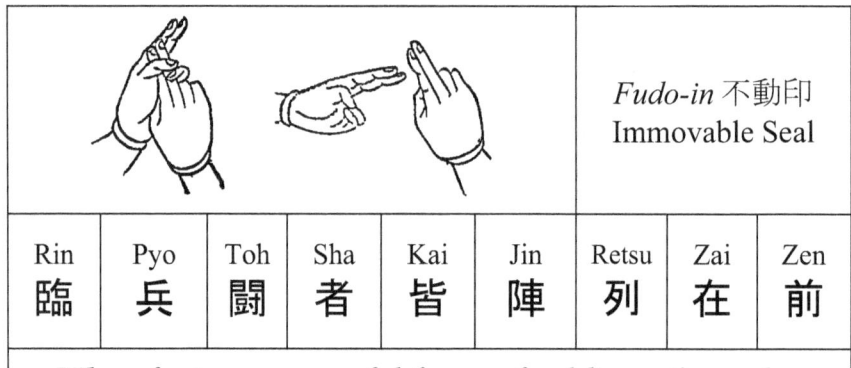

Rin	Pyo	Toh	Sha	Kai	Jin	Retsu	Zai	Zen
臨	兵	鬭	者	皆	陣	列	在	前

When facing a powerful force of soldiers, those that seek to fight all break ranks and move to the vanguard.

First make the Immovable Seal. Then, as your horse is walking pour all your devotion into the Kuji as you chant aloud or silently and, when you reach the final Kanji Zen 前 Before, focus on tightening that last Kanji.[71] This will immediately secure your horse as if you have lashed it in place. This method is similar to the previously introduced method of securing your enemy's sword so that he cannot draw it from his scabbard.

---

[71] A different Kuji book recommends,
While using the Two-Sword Seal, press out with your ring fingers, while pushing inward with your thumbs, creating a strong pressure as if tightening.

右手ニテ刀印　臨兵闘者皆陣列在前

右ハ馬ノ歩足ニ中テ九ノ字ヲ誦シ前字ニテ卯ヲ強クシムル也。此卯ハ無名指ニテ大指ヲ押ヘナリ

一大指ニテ中指ヲシムル。而メ右ノ如ク九ノ字ヲ誦ノ前字ニテ卯ヲシムル也。青龍結奥ノ卯ト云ナリ

下馬落之大事

馬ニ向テ九ノ字ヲ切ハ。大刀馬驚テ人

Ware Joba wo Tsunagi-ho 吾乗馬を繋法
How to Secure the Horse You are Riding On

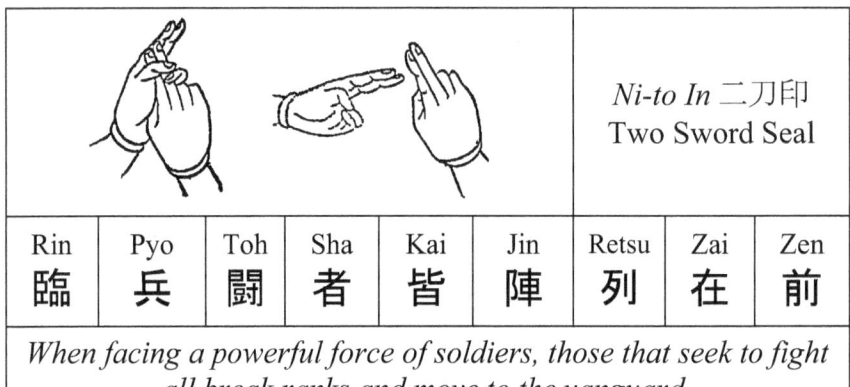

						Ni-to In 二刀印 Two Sword Seal		
Rin	Pyo	Toh	Sha	Kai	Jin	Retsu	Zai	Zen
臨	兵	闘	者	皆	陣	列	在	前
When facing a powerful force of soldiers, those that seek to fight all break ranks and move to the vanguard.								

First make the Two Sword Seal. Then, as the horse is walking, chant the entirely of the Kuji. Finally, as you reach the last Kanji Zen 前, Before, focus on that Kanji as if you are tightening it. While using the Two-Sword Seal, press out with your ring fingers, while pushing inward with your thumbs, creating a strong pressure as if tightening.

Alternate Method

First, tuck your right thumb against your palm and grip it with your middle finger. Then close your other fingers into a fist.[72]

Next go through the Kuji as previously described and focus strongly on the Kanji Zen, creating a strong pressure as if tightening.

This will form the *Seiryu Kekkai no In* 青龍結界の印 Blue Dragon Ward protecting the area around you.

---

[72] There was no illustration of this seal, it is based on the description.

一、落馬スルナリ

一、鞘縛ノ法ヲ行ヘハ、人ト馬シバラル也、而メ右手ヲ叙卯ニテ四ニ竪五ニ横ニ切ルベシ、必ス落馬スルナリ

一、人ノ馬ニ向テ、極秘結裹ノ九ノ字ヲ切ル、中点ヲ馬ニウツナリ、下馬落ノ最モ也

一、下馬札ノ事、九字ト、二十八ノ宿ト、三十六ノ禽ヲ以テ法ヲ立ルアリ、曾我氏ノ傳ナリ、別書アリ署レ之

一、馬場氏ヨリ傳來ノ下馬札書法アリ、馬字ヲ九ノ字ニ中ル、九、九、八十一ノ理ヲ以テス。今コヽニ記ス

Geba Ochi no Daiji 下馬落之大事
An Important Lesson: How to Make Someone Fall off a Horse

If you do Kuji while facing a horse it will generally startle them and cause the rider to fall.

Using Kuji to Lock Your Opponent's Sword in His Sheath

If you use the previously mentioned *Saya-Shibari*, How to Lock Your Opponent's Sword in His Sheath you will be able to bind both horse and rider together.

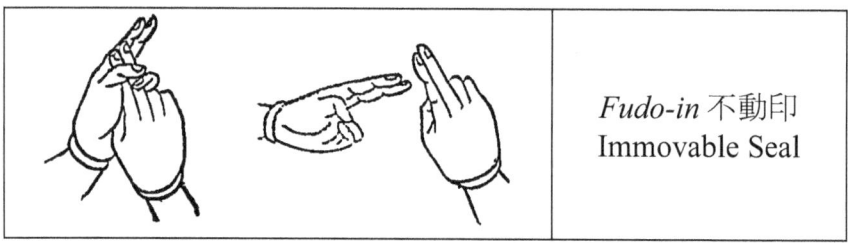

Fudo-in 不動印
Immovable Seal

This technique begins by chanting *Saki* 先, meaning First, while making the Immovable Seal. After chanting, use the Ken-in, Sword Seal, in your right hand to cut the Four Horizontal and Five Vertical Lines. This will invariable cause the rider to fall from his horse.

Make a Rider Fall From His Horse

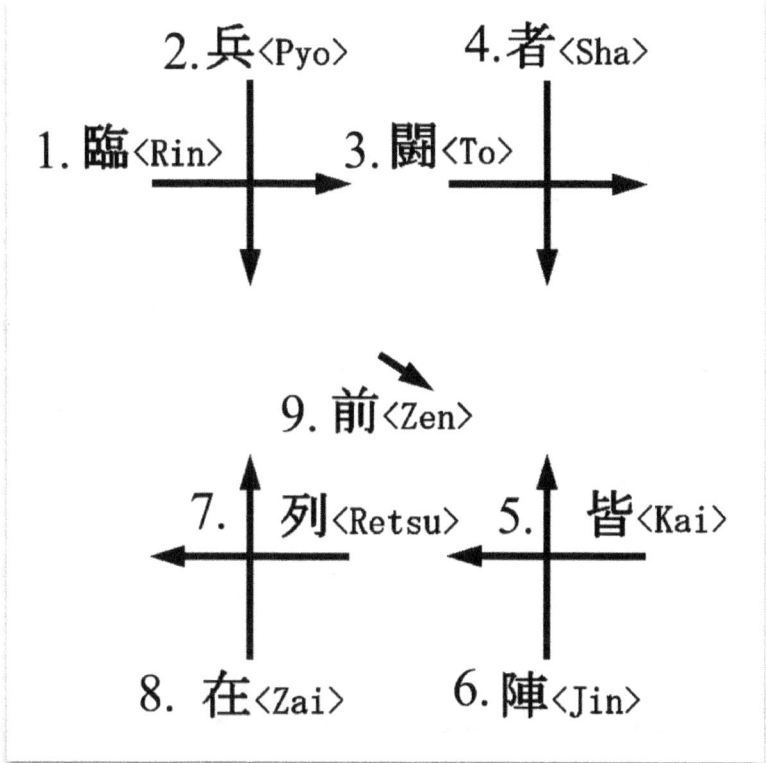

To do this, face the horse and cut the Kuji as indicated by the chart below. The final cut is in the center and should be directed directly at the horse. This will cause a rider to fall from his horse.

Gebafuta no Koto 下馬札の事
Sign saying you must dismount your horse and proceed on foot[73]

Regarding *Gebafuta*, signs saying you must dismount your horse and proceed on foot. There is a method for crafting one of these signs that combines Kuji with the Twenty-Eight Mansions along with the Thirty-Six Creatures. This is a teaching handed down through the Soga Clan.[74] Since it is part of a separate document it will not be included here.

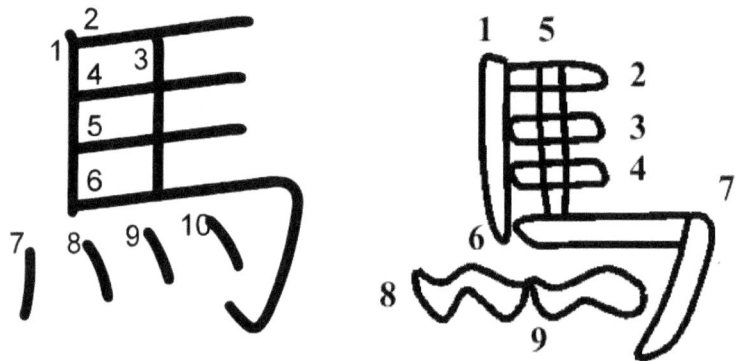

Left: Standard way to write the Kanji Horse
Right: Writing Horse with nine strokes.

There is a method of constructing a *Gebafuta* sign, transmitted by a man named Mr. Baba.[75] It is a method whereby the Kanji *Uma* 馬, horse is written with nine strokes instead of ten so it can be used in the Kuji.

This method of construction is based on the principle that nine times nine is eighty-one.

---

[73] These signs would be placed near busy intersections or in front of small bridges or any place caution was needed when crossing.

[74] The Soga clan were aristocrats in the Asuka Era (538 ~710) They were influential in government policy and helped spread Buddhism in Japan.

[75] The name Baba 馬場 contains the Kanji horse + place.

The Kanji 八十一 Eight + Ten + One can refer just to individual numbers but they can also be seen as indicating "eight tens plus one" or eighty-one. The method will be described on the following page.

Translator's Note:
Sanjurokkin 三十六禽 **The Thirty-Six Creatures**
A day was divided into twelve two-hour segment of time and used for divination purposes.

1. 鼠 Rat	2. 豺 Mountain Dog	3. 牛 Cow
4. 蟹 Crab	5. 鼈 River Turtle	6. 狸 Raccoon Dog
7. 豹 Leopard	8. 虎 Tiger	9. 狐 Fox
10. 兔 Rabbit	11. 狢 Serpent	12. 龍 Dragon
13. 鮫 Shark	14. 魚 Fish	15. 蝉 Cicadia
16. 蛆 Maggot	17. 蛇 Snake	18. 鹿 Deer
19. 馬 Horse	20. 猝 Deer	21. 羊 Sheep
22. 雁 Goose	23. 鷹 Hawk	24. 狖 Weasel
25. 猿 Monkey	26. 猴 Wild Monkey	27. 烏 Bird
28. 鶏 Rooster	29. 雉 Pheasant	30. 狗 Wild Dog
31. 狼 Wolf	32. 豺 Mountain Dog	33. 獐 Wild Dog
34. 猶 Dragon Dog	35. 猪 Wild Pig	36. 燕 Swallow

下馬

馬字九畫九ノ字ニ中ルヽ也
文字ノ大サ三寸ニ過ベカラズ。且札ノ
寸法アリ。別ニ記シ置モノナリ。書法
ハ家ノ秘事ナリ

札

八十一

How to Make a *Gebafuta*, a sign saying you must dismount your horse and proceed on foot

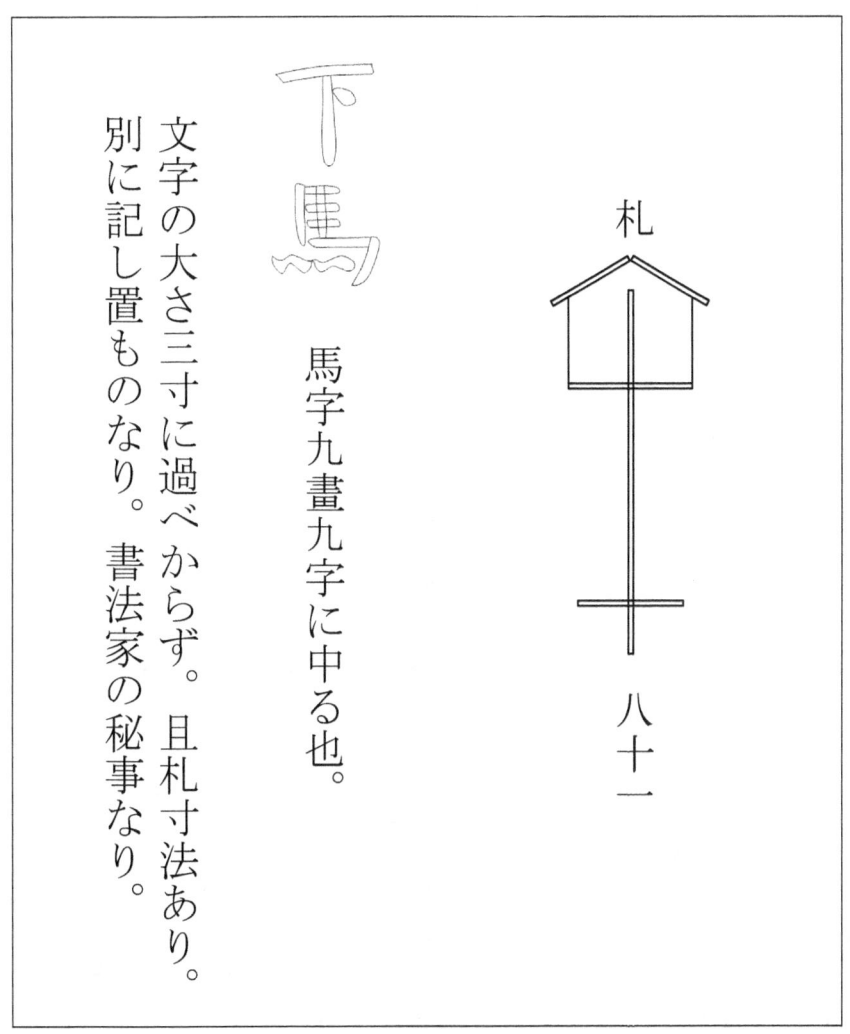

How to Make a *Gebafuta*, a sign saying you must dismount your horse and proceed on foot

When writing the Kanji horse, the lettering should not be bigger than 3 Sun, 9 cm/3 inches. In addition, there are specific instructions regarding the dimensions of the sign. However, this is a separate teaching. This is a secret of calligraphers.

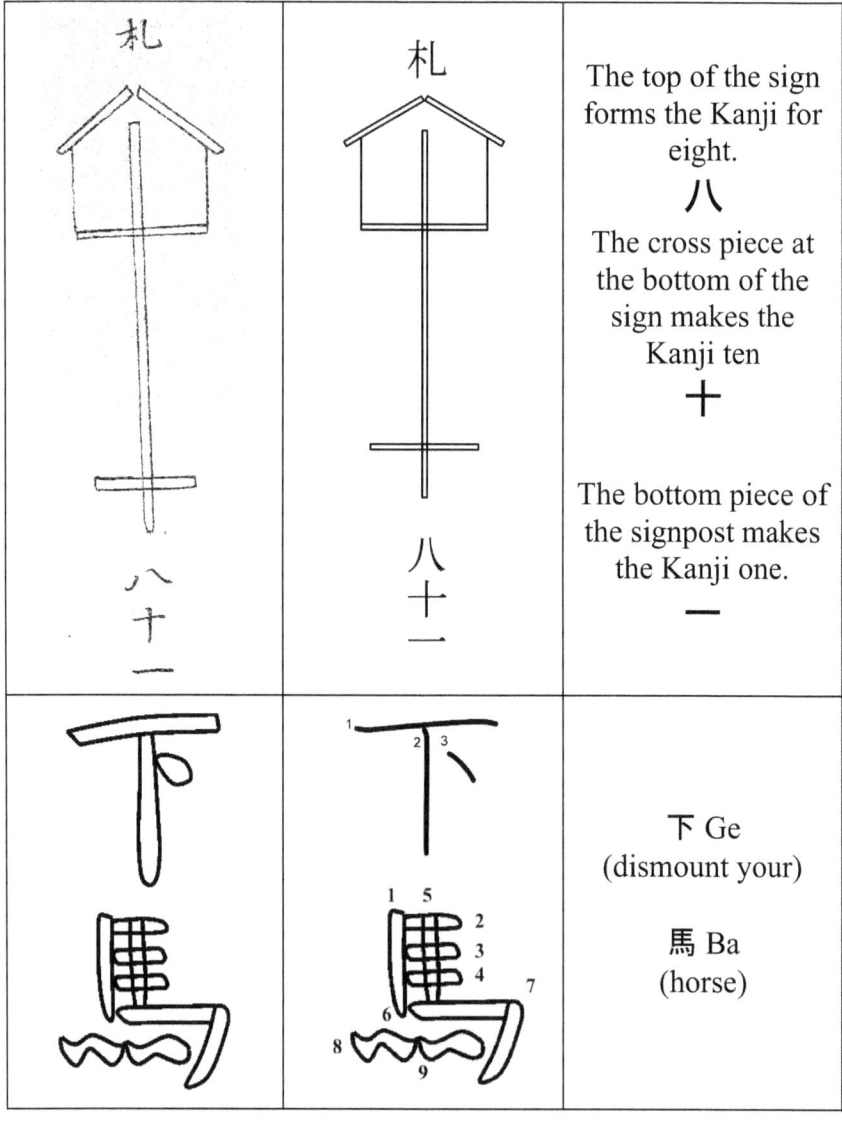

催生之符ノ大事
此法ハ如何ナル難産ニテモ無相違。
湯水又ハ箸バカリニテモ呑スナリ。
男子ハ左、女子ハ右ノ手ニ握テ生ル。
則取テ川ヘ流スベシ
十一二月ニ取タル兎ノ脳ヲ陰干ニ
シテ置キ用。右兎ノ脳ヲ少シ墨ニ和
ノ。妙字ヲ九ノ字ニ中テ畫ス。亦右ノ
兎脳ヲ白紙ニ塗テ陰干シ置テ用
モ可ナリ。用ル時ハ方ニ切テ妙字
ヲ右ノ如ク筆スベシ。而メ之ヲ九
メ呑スナリ

妙

Saisei no Futa no Daiji 催生之符の大事
An Important Lesson: A Talisman For When a Woman Feels Birthing Pangs

This method is incomparable when dealing with a difficult birth. All that is required is drawing this talisman on a piece of paper and swallowing it or dissolving it in hot water before drinking.

If the woman gives birth to a boy, he will be holding it in his left fist. If she gives birth to a girl, the girl will be holding it in her right fist. You should take it out of the baby's hand and cast it into the river.

Alternate Method

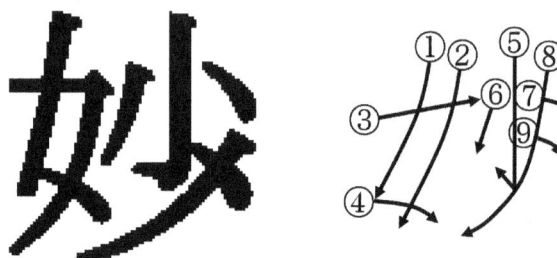

Catch a rabbit in the twelfth month of the year. Dry the brain thoroughly in a shady spot. Take the previously mentioned dried rabbit brain and mix it with a little ink until it makes a paste you can write with. Then use that ink to make a talisman by writing the Kanji *Myo* 妙 which has been adjusted to have nine strokes and therefore represents the entirety of the Kuji.

Another way to make this talisman is to smear the previously mentioned rabbit brain on a piece of white paper and dry it in the shade. When you need to use the spell, cut the paper to the proper dimensions and draw the Kanji *Myo* 妙 as was previously described. After that roll the paper up and swallow it.

Note that this talisman should not be used until the final month of pregnancy or it will cause a miscarriage. There are other ill effects as well. Understand that this method should not be used for anything other than difficult births. Failing to abide by this will mean you will receive divine retribution.

一、此等ハ月不足ノ用ハ流産ス。左ナク此害アリ。臨ノ産ニテモ難産ノ外用ユベカラズ。天ノ答ヲ受ベシ

託物ヲ離ス大事
人ニ物ノ託シ一物ニ非。狸格ノ類。
凡獣ニ限ラズ。虫ナド。人ノ死生ノ靈。
其種々アリ。能木ニ上ル物ノ託ヲトル云。
高ニ上ラザル狐ト云。物ノ
人ハ大ニ推骨ヲ押メ着レバ。額ニ粟粒
ノ如キ吹出モノ見ル也。唇邊ニシコ
リ有リ。旦常ニ唾ヲ事ナクメ吐人ハ。

Kotozukaru[76] *wo Hanasu Daiji* 託物を離す大事
How to Free Yourself From Another's Control

There are many different ways to fall under the control of another. You could become possessed not only by animals, such as foxes, raccoon dogs, and badgers, but also by insects or the spirits of the dead. There are a multitude of possibilities which include Yakan, which are adept at climbing trees.[77] Creatures that look similar but do not climb up high into trees are known as Kitsune, foxes.

---

[76] *Kotozukaru* 託物 is another way to say *Tsuki Mono* 憑物 an evil spirit that possesses a person.

[77] A *Yakan* 野干 is a trickster animal often described in Chinese texts. It was originally a Jackal in India, and by the time the word made it to Japan, it was used to describe either a fox or a mountain dog. In particular any creature that resembles a fox and is good at climbing trees. In addition, folk magicians would listen to the howl of these creatures to determine future good or bad luck. In Japan, early as 1201 AD a Yakan (fox or foxlike creature) was accused of causing a person to forget the location of a famous sword.

Illustration of a Yakan (here labeled a jackal) as well as its skull. By Minakata Kumagusu 南方熊楠 (1867 ~ 1941)

If you suspect a person has been possessed by a fox, press down on the bones at the base of the neck. If you do this, small bumps the size of grains of millet will appear on their forehead as if blown by the wind, then they are possessed.[78]

It is important to note that if a person who usually doesn't spit, begins spitting while walking along the road, it is usually the result of that person being controlled by an insect.

---

[78] *A person possessed by a fox will have a bluish-black tint to their skin and small bumps both above and between the eyebrows as if grains of millet have been blown on the face. If the skin around the patient's mouth is tight then they are possessed by a fox.*
  -*A Secret Guide to Employing Supernatural Methods*
  実験調法神術霊妙秘蔵書
  Karasawa Shokaku 柄沢照覚
  1981

大方虫ノ記タルセ。凡人生テ七日ノ内ニ物來テ先メ肉ル。其物ハ其人一生ノ禁物トナル。赤胞衣ヲ七日ノ内ニ能守ルベシ。若物アッテ胞衣ヲ犯セバ。夫人生レテ其物又一生ノ禁物トナル。故ニ七日ノ七日ニメ真ノ氣全ク固ル也。是ヲ以テ物有内ハ真ノ元定ラサル也。是ヲ以テ物有テ犯ヲ得タリ。貴人ニテハ守若結家ノ護身ノ一ニ非下人ニテモハ種字守ベキ種字モアルベキ種字也。右ノ如ク記ベキ孤ノ記モ。右ノ如ク記ベキ因レリ。左モナキニ人ルニハ中々記ニナド逢ノ理ナシ。天狗ニ狐ルル類、夜妖一物ニ逢

It is said that in the first seven days of a person's life, a thing will come and try and take possession of you. That thing, no matter what kind of creature, will become something forbidden to you and your greatest weakness for the rest of your life.

The reason for this is because it takes seven days for a child's true Ki, or spirit, to become completely solidified. Therefore, during that seven day period, it is essential that parents are vigilant about keeping their baby wrapped securely in a blanket. If a creature[79] violates the borders of your home and immerses itself in your baby's blanket, that will be the cause of an eternal weakness for your child.

As I mentioned before, it takes seven days for a child's true Ki, or spirit, to become completely solidified. What this means is the child's True Nature has not been determined.[80] Thus, supernatural creatures use that interval to take control of a child.

This is why it is important for all people to protect themselves with talismans and protective wards. This is not something that is limited to people of noble birth, even people of lowly birth must be careful.

In conclusion, the reason a fox can assert its control over a person is because there was the seed of possibility for taking control over them. Similarly, if you are clawed by a Tengu, mountain goblin, you will later no doubt be tormented by Yokai, ghosts and demons, at night. On the other hand, a fox will not be able to possess a person who is completely protected

Thus there is always a root cause to the problem of possession. However, for the most part people are possessed by foxes. Though Yakan should be thought of as also playing a major role in possessing people in addition to foxes. The fox is a supernatural creature dedicated to causing misfortune in humans.[81] The supernatural power of foxes only increases as they age.

---

[79] This is referring to *Chimi-Moryo* 魑魅魍魎 evil spirits of rivers and mountains as well as foxes, tanuki and insects.

[80] Shingen 眞元 True origin.

[81] Yoshin 妖神 evil god or god of misfortune.

ナドニ右ノ理ニ因レリ。其中ニモ多ク人ニ託ハ狐ニ十リ。モシ狐ト野云狐ハ妖神十リ。年老テ益靈アリ。彼ガ喪ルル所ハ別稻荷大明神。花山院是ナリ。精クハニ記シ置者十リ。

一、病人ノ常ニ著用シタル衣類ヲ壇ニ置テ之ニ向テ七日九字ヲ行フベシ。最行者ハ結界ノ後ニ取カヽルナリ。

一、虎骨辰砂和メ。左ノ内ニ前字ヲ九字ニ中テ畫ス。握リ固テ其病家ニ入ル也。若病人ニ能名作ノ腰物ヲ帯ス。之ニテ四ニ継五ニ横ノ九ノ字ヲ切ベケシラバ。

The only place a fox fears is *Inari no Daimyojin*, any shrine dedicated to Inari as well as the Temple of the Flower Mountain. I will describe this in detail in a later section.[82]

- The sick person's daily clothes should be placed on the altar. Do the Kuji every day for seven days while facing the clothing on the altar. However, the Kuji practitioner should not begin until a boundary ward has been formed.

- Form the boundary before entering the person's house. Do this by mixing tiger bone and dragon sand (cinnabar,) and drawing the Kanji *Zen* 前 on your left palm. This single Kanji represents the entirely of the Kuji. Squeeze your hand tightly into a fist as you enter the sick person's house. You should wear a sword made by a fine craftsman on your waist.[83]

- If the patient should become overly excited or violent, use that blade to cut the Four Vertical and Five Horizontal lines. It is important that the blade you use is extremely sharp. Even if you own a sword made by a famous swordsmith, if it is dull it will not be effective.

---

[82] *Inari Okami* 稲荷大神 is one of the principal kami of Shinto. Inari is the Kami of foxes, fertility, rice, tea and sake, agriculture and industry along with general prosperity and worldly success. In earlier Japan, Inari was also the patron of swordsmiths and merchants. Inari appears to have been worshipped since the founding of a shrine at Inari Mountain in 711 AD.
Hanayama no In 花山の院 also known as Hanayama Inari Shrine is a Shinto shrine located in Kyoto. It is named after Emperor Kazan 花山天皇 (968 ~ 1008) who retired there. The shrine is said to have been founded in 903 by the order of Emperor Daigo. The "Inari Mound" within the shrine is said to be the place where Sanjo Munechika forged the famous sword *Kogumaru* 小狐丸 Small Fox Blade, by the divine power of Inari in the 12th century AD.
[83] This is probably referring to a short sword or knife in a scabbard without a Tsuba, hand-guard.

如何ニモ好キレ物豆、名作ニテモ鈍テ物ハ用ニ不足ナリ

一、龍骨虎骨辰砂ヲ和合ノ井花水ヲ以テ、井田ノ折形ヲ調テ、病人ノ居間ノ四方ニ押スナリ

一、白雞頭花ノ楊枝形。長九一寸ナルヲ持テ、病人ノ面ヲ見合スベシ。九字ヲ念誦スベシ。狐ナラバ、必面ヲ見合ケス。面ヲ嫌テ脇ヲ視ルベシ。其目ヲ、タル所ニ右ノ楊枝形ヲササシ止ベシ。

一、病人ヲ動カアタハサル也

一、病人ヲ敷物ニ乗セ。四方ニ一寸ノ香ヲ

- Mix powdered dragon bone (mammal fossil,) tiger bone and dragon sand (cinnabar) with Flower Well Water (water drawn from the well between the hours of the Ox and Tiger 2:00 ~ 4:00 a.m.) Fold four pieces of paper into the well-field shape 井 and use the above mixture to draw the Kuji. Paste one on each of the four walls of the sick person's main living area.

- Pluck a white flower from a cockscomb trim it until it is shaped like a toothpick, about 9 Sun, 3.5 inches/9 centimeters, long.[84] While facing the sick person focus all your energy on doing the Kuji. If the patient is actually under a fox's control, the fox spirit will recoil at facing you directly and will look to the side. Thus you should use the previously described toothpick shaped flower to prevent the patient from looking away from you.

---

[84] Celosia argentea, the plumed cockscomb, is famous for its bright coloring. In India and China it is known as a troublesome weed.

- Place the sick person on a rug, mix *Issun Ko* purifying powdered incense with ink.[85] Use this to draw the four vertical and five horizontal lines representing the Kuji. You can also use a single Kanji such as Tiger, Mysterious, or Before.

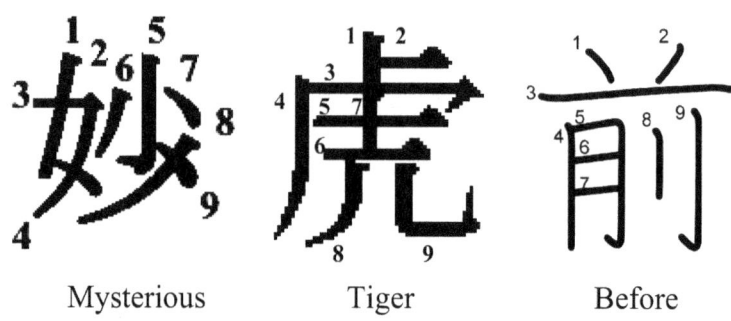

Mysterious   Tiger   Before

Any *Kyukaku Kuji* 九画, Nine-stroke Kanji can be used to represent all nine Kanji of the Kuji.

---

[85] *Issun-ko* 一寸香 literally "1 inch/3 centimeter Incense" or "purifying powdered incense" is another way of saying *Zuko* 塗香 the practice of applying incense to a Buddha's statue or the body of a practitioner to cleanse impurities and keep evil spirits away.

Another word for this is Nuriko 塗香 *a generic term for powdered incense that is applied to the body.* Nuriko *is made from sandalwood* 白檀, *agarwood* 沈木 *and Dragon Brain (borneol,) In esoteric Buddhist temples, such as those of the Shingon sect,* Nuriko *is used to purify the body and mind before a Buddhist memorial service.* Nuriko *is applied to the body, mouth, and chest to purify them before touching Buddhist ritual objects. Some temples in Konoyama place* Nuriko *at the entrance to the main hall to encourage visitors to cleanse their bodies and renew their minds to face the Buddha; they simply take a pinch of* Nuriko, *rub it all over their hands, and make a gesture of applying the incense to their chest, mouth, and forehead, and they are done.*

-The World of the Walking Pilgrimage
お遍路で生まれ変わる〜歩き遍路の世界〜

This incense is available by mail order.

墨ニ和メ、之ヲ以テ四ノ縦五ノ横ノ九ノ字ヲ書ス。亦虎字。或ハ妙字。又ハ前号ヲ九畫九ノ字ニ中テ書スモ可ナリ

一ス香之方

龍骨　虎骨　白雞頭花　安息香
乳香　以上五種末メ用ルナリ。一方
ニ降真香ヲ加ルアリ。等分量ナリ

又方

狐ノ尾　白尾先ノ用
安息香　以上四ノ種最モ別々ニ黒燒
ニメ。而メ共ニ合用。一方ニ茸松香ト
忍冬ノ末ヲ加フ。等分量ナリ

Issun Ko no Kata 一寸香之方
How to prepare *Issun Ko* purifying powdered incense
Warrior Household Method

This is a combination of the following five ingredients: Powdered dragon bone (fossilized bones of a mammal,) tiger bone, white cockscomb flower, serenity incense, [86] and frankincense. [87] In addition, some people add powdered sandalwood incense.[88] These should all be powdered in equal amounts.

How to prepare *Issun Ko* purifying powdered incense
Taoist Method

Combine the following five ingredients: Hair from a fox's tail, specifically the white hairs on the end of the tail,[89] the fang of a wolf, white cockscomb flower and Serenity Incense. Each of the four should be burned until they form charcoal, powdered and then combined together.

Some versions of this recipe also mix in equal parts powdered Sweet Pine Incense[90] and Enduring Winter.[91]

---

[86] *Ansoku Ko* 安息香 Benzoinis a balsamic resin obtained from the bark of several species of trees in the genus Styrax. It is used as incense and medicine.

[87] *Nyu Ko* 乳香 Frankincense, It is believed to have been introduced to Japan via the Silk Road in the 10th century, as descriptions of incense prescriptions appeared in Japan in the 10th century.

[88] *Ko-shin Ko* 降真香 Sandalwood incense.

[89] There is also a plant called *Kitsune no Shippo* 狐尻尾 "fox tail" which is more commonly known as stag's-horn clubmoss. It is widely used as a medical herb.

[90] *Kansho Ko* 甘松香 Spikenard, also called muskroot, is an aromatic amber-colored essential oil.

[91] *Nindo* 忍冬 Japanese honeysuckle. It is often grown as an ornamental plant, but has become an invasive species in a number of countries. In folk medicine it is used to treat gonorrhea.

又方

熊野牛ノ王ノ黒燒　降真香　茸松ノ香
乳香　安息香

以上五種等分末メ用ルナリ是等ノ方皆一家ノ秘傳ナリ中ノ一方ハ抓ヨリ相傳ナリ。精ク八別ニ記ス。始ノ一方ハ兵家ノ傳ナリ。終ノ一方ハ佛家傳ナリ

一兵家傳佛家傳道家傳ノ三方ノ一ス香ノ内兵家ハ有形ノ物ニ用レバ勝レテ靈アリ。佛家ハ無形ノ物ニ用レバ勝テ靈アリ。道家ハ抓ニ用テ宜シ。最モ皆常ニ帶テ害ヲ除クナリ。抓ヨリ相

How to prepare *Issun Ko* purifying powdered incense Buddhist Method

A charred Talisman of the Ox-Headed Heavenly King from a Kumano Shrine, [92] Sandalwood incense, Sweet Pine incense, Frankincense Incense, and Serenity incense. Powder the above five ingredients in equal parts and mix them together.

There are many ways to prepare this mixture and each school has their own secret method. One of them says that the original recipe was handed down from a fox. I will cover this in detail later, for now I will introduce two other methods. The first is from a military family and the second is a Buddhist tradition.

---

[92] *Gozu Tennō* 牛頭天王 "Ox-Headed Heavenly King" is a Japanese deity of disease and healing. Originally imported to Japan from China, the Ox-Headed Heavenly King is regarded as both as a causer of and protector against epidemics. The talismans (pictured below) are also known as *Karasu Go-O* 烏牛王, Crow Ox King, since they are written with "crow-letters." It is not clear if the author means to burn one of these talismans or some sort of medical herb or incense sold at one of the many Kumano Shines where these talismans are made.

There are three ways to prepare *Issun Ko* purifying powdered incense. The first was the Warrior Household Tradition, the second was the Taoist tradition and the last was the Buddhist tradition.

The Warrior Household Tradition is best used with tangible objects, due to the powerful manifestation of spiritual energy granted after prayer. The Buddhist Household Tradition, is best when used on intangible things, due to the powerful manifestation of spiritual energy granted after prayer. The Taoist Household Tradition is particularly effective on foxes. You should carry all three on your person to remove the chance of terrible misfortune.

It is said the method from the Taoist Tradition is the one originally taught to a Taoist by a fox.

一 傳ヲ道家傳トスルナリ
一 病人ヲ捕ヘテ九字ヲ念誦シ。一す一香
ヲ子ニ塗テ。ヒ子ノリニハルベシ。若狐
ナドニテ有バ脇ノ下ヘ木方カタテ
リヲヒ子ヨリ出スナリ。一す一香ヲ
和メ。其カタテニ輪ヲ墨ニテ九字ヲ
書メ。其カタレニモ三モピ子ヨリ出ス
咒絶フナカアリ皆其如クモシ而メ折角ニ
ヒテル丁ナリ。終ニ起シトモ云ハ。堅ク
定テ誓約ヲ取ル。究所ハ稲荷大ノ明神
殿花山院殿ナリ。而メ一足ニ病人ヲ
蹴倒スナリ。後ニ千足ノ大ノ指ノ仇ノ際

How to use *Issun Ko* purifying powdered incense

Take hold of the patient, focus your energy and chant the Kuji. Place some *Issun Ko* purifying powdered incense in your palm and stir it around. Generally speaking, if you suspect a young fox has possessed the patient, scoop up a lump of the *Issun Ko* purifying powdered incense and press it under the armpit.

Next, thin the *Issun Ko* purifying powdered incense with a little ink and draw a circle around the lump of incense under the patient's armpit. As you do this you should be continuously chanting the Kuji. This process can be repeated two or three times. Each repetition should be done in the same way, by first making a ball of *Issun Ko* purifying powdered incense and pressing it under the armpit before drawing a circle around it with the ink-incense mixture. Finally, bend at an angle.[93]

When you have finished this spell, the fox or whatever supernatural creature that has taken over the patient will say,

Koko Kara Tachi Saru
I will leave this place

The moment the creature says this you have formed a secure binding contract. A connection is formed with the Great Divine Fox Shrine or the former residence of Emperor Kazan.[94] Then kick the patient down with one foot.

---

[93] *Sekkaku* 折角 To break the corner of something. It is not clear what the author means, however it may be "Bend the patient's elbows and wrists to about 90°" or "rub the sick person's body as hard as you can."

[94] Hanayama Inari Shrine is a Shinto shrine located in Kyoto. It is where the Emperor Kazan 花山天皇 (968 ~ 1008) retired.

一病人ニ七五三壯灸スベシ是ヲ狐落シノ法ト云・平愈メ符ヲ常ニ懐中スベシ・其法後ニ記ス

一病人ニ一寸香ヲ呑スベシ・或ハ燒テ薰ブベシ・敷物ノ甲方ニ右云如ク九一字ヲ畫メ病人ノ不動・真劔ヲ以テ四竪五一横ニ九字ヲ切ル・病人タケラバ幣ヲ以テサスベシ
幣之寸法

鏡竪九一寸 幣竪九一寸 内切幣一寸八分
横三寸六分 無横二寸七一分

Later, you should treat the area with moxibustion, burning mugwort, at the cuticle of the thumbs of your hands and big toes of your feet in *Shichi-Go-San*, Seven-Five-Three, style.[95] This method is called *Kitsune Otoshi*, toppling the fox, or removing any spell placed on you by a fox. After you are healed, you should carry a talisman in your breast pocked at all times. I will describe how to make this talisman in a later section.

---

[95] This means to either burn mugwort either three, five or seven times. *Shichi-Go-San* 七五三 "seven-five-three" is a traditional Japanese rite of passage and festival day for three- and seven-year-old girls, five-year-old and sometimes three-year-old boys, held annually on November 15 to celebrate the growth and well-being of young children. The ceremony began in the Kamakura period (1185 ~1333.) The ages 3, 5 and 7 are odd numbers and considered lucky. Note that when children are born they are considered to be one year old. The numbers 3, 5 and 7 appear on the corners of the *Kimon Tonkotsu* 奇門遁甲 ancient divination board.

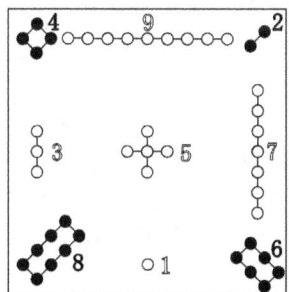

The ceremony takes place on the 15th day of the 11th month. The 11th month is when the harvest is done and offerings are made to the gods in thanks. According to the twenty-eight lunar mansions the 15th is a day that the devil is not waking about the earth.

How to use *Issun Ko* purifying powdered incense: Alternates

A sick person should drink *Issun Ko* purifying powdered incense. Alternately they can burn the incense and inhale the smoke.

Draw the Kuji, as previously described, on the four corners of the mat the patient is laying on. Tell the patient not to move as you do this. Next, draw your sword and cut the Four Vertical and Five Horizontal Lines. If the sick person becomes violent, strike him with a *Hei* 幣 a Shinto staff tied with folded paper streamers.

Dimensions of the Hei, Shinto Staff and streamers

Hei no Sunpo 幣之寸法
Measurements of the staff and streamers.

Kagami 鏡 Mirror
Cut a piece of paper that is 9 Sun, 11 inches/27 cm, tall and 3.6 Sun, 4.3 in/11 cm wide.

Shisui 四睡
Cut a piece of paper 9 Sun, 11 inches/27 cm, tall with cuts 1.8 Sun 2.1 inches/ 5.4 centimeters, deep every 2.7 Sun 3.2 inches/8 centimeters.

Translator's Note: How to make the paper streamers

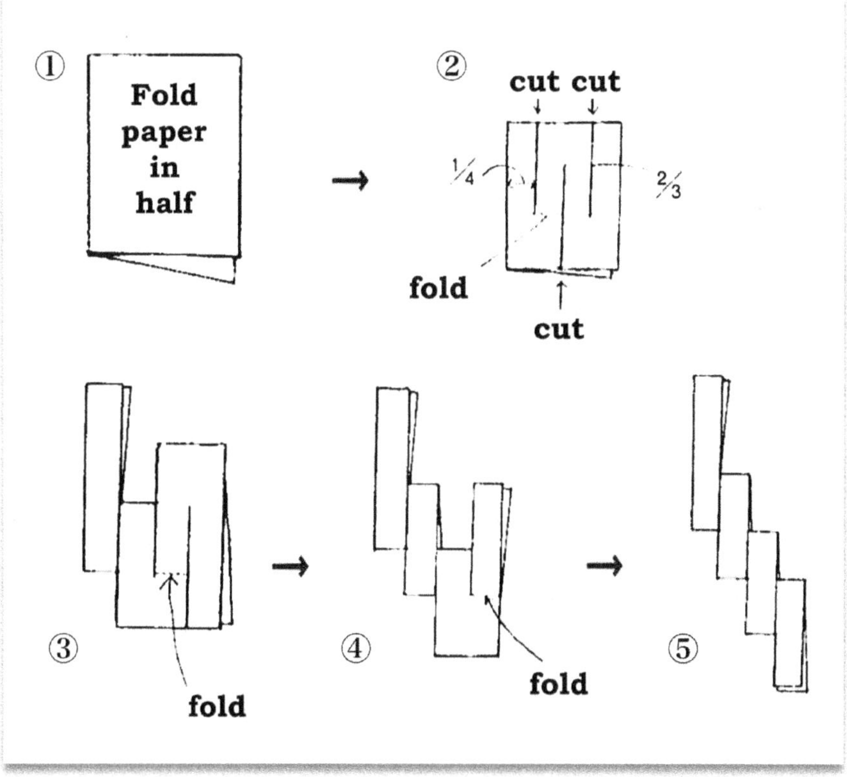

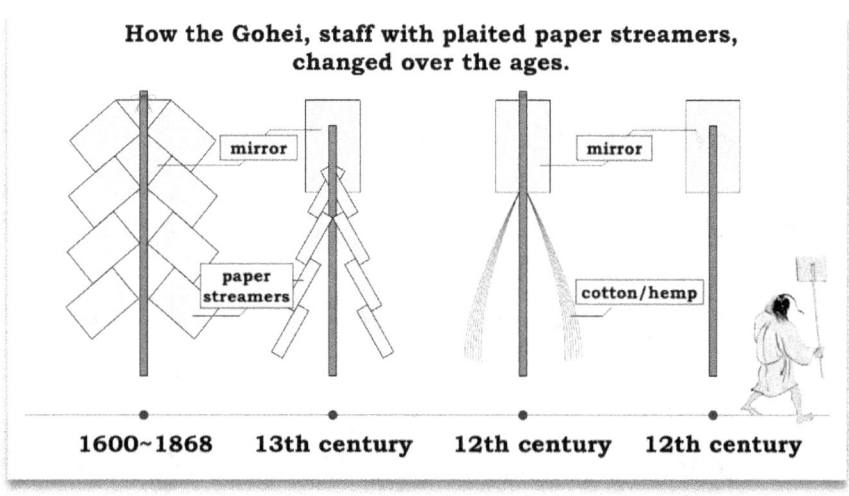

一　壇法式

先ツ壇ヲ莊テ八方ニ七五三ヲ引ベシ。九尺八方十ナリ。南面ニ莊ルナリ。テ九八十一枚ナリ。右鏡九枚。左右八毎七十二枚。共ニ合串長三尺六寸ヲ以テ用ユ竹紙九枚

壇板。八方毎方九寸。厚九分。足八方毎方九分。高二尺七寸。四本ヲ用ルナリ。壇ノ八方ニ幡ヲ立之。中央ニ常建。壇ニ臨ミ兵闘者皆陣列在ノ結裏九字式ヲ畫ス幣ハ則前ニ中ルナリ。幡八字ヲ竿九寸。幡錦竪九寸。横九分キリ

Bamboo Pole

The bamboo pole should be 3 Shaku 6 Sun, 3.6 feet/ 109 cm. The pole should be made of Bamboo Grass.[96] There should be nine paper streamers.

Mirrors

There should be nine mirrors in front with an additional seventy-two mirrors hanging in strings of eight on the left and right. This means there should be eighty-one in all.

Altar

First build an altar and mount a *Shichi-Go-San Shime* a Seven-Five-Three Enclosing Rope[97] should be drawn in all around it/ in all directions. It should make a circle 9 Shaku, 8.8 feet/2.7 meters, across. The alter should be built facing south.

---

[96] *Suzutake* 篠竹 bamboo grass.

[97] The general term for an enclosing rope is *Shime* which are made out of rice straw. In this case the text refers to a *Shichi-Go-San Nawa* 七五三縄, or Seven-Five-Three Enclosing Rope. In this case the entire four Kanji combination is simply read as "Shime Nawa." The ropes are used for ritual purification in Shinto.

The seven tassels hanging from it are said to be the seven generations of Tenjin deities, the five tassels the five generations of Jishin deities, and the three tassels the three generations of Hyuga (Miyagi Prefecture) deities. Odd numbers are considered to be yang numbers and are said to prevent bad Yin Ki from entering the area where the deities reside.

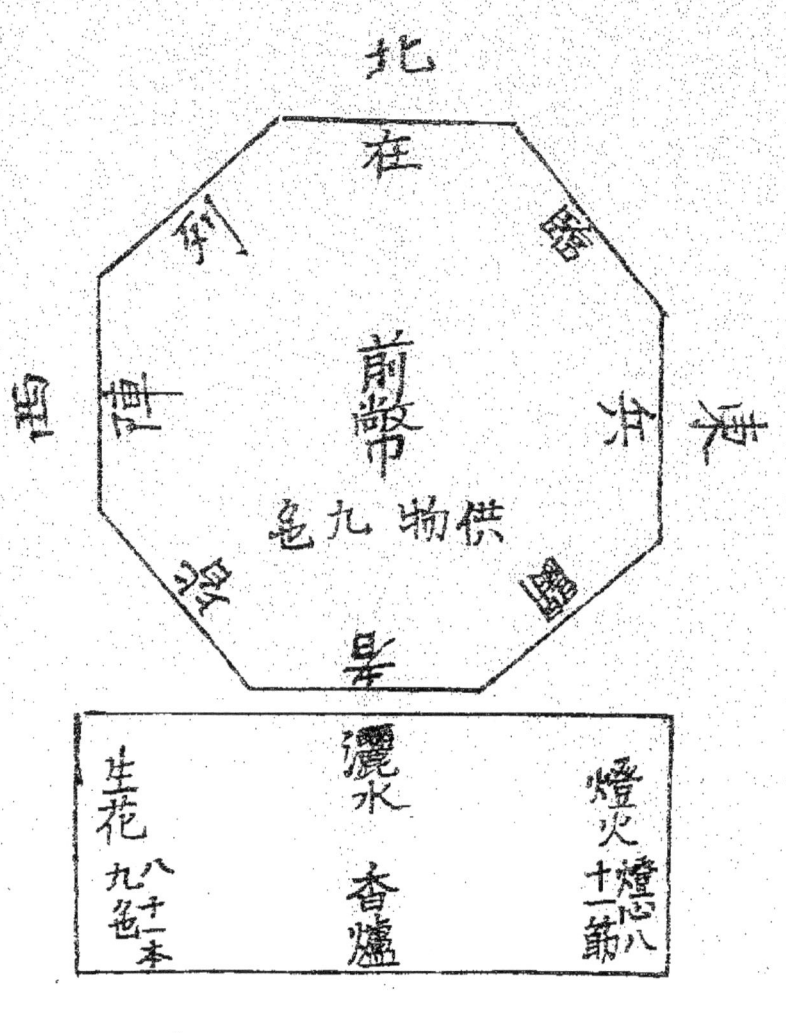

Transcription of Altar

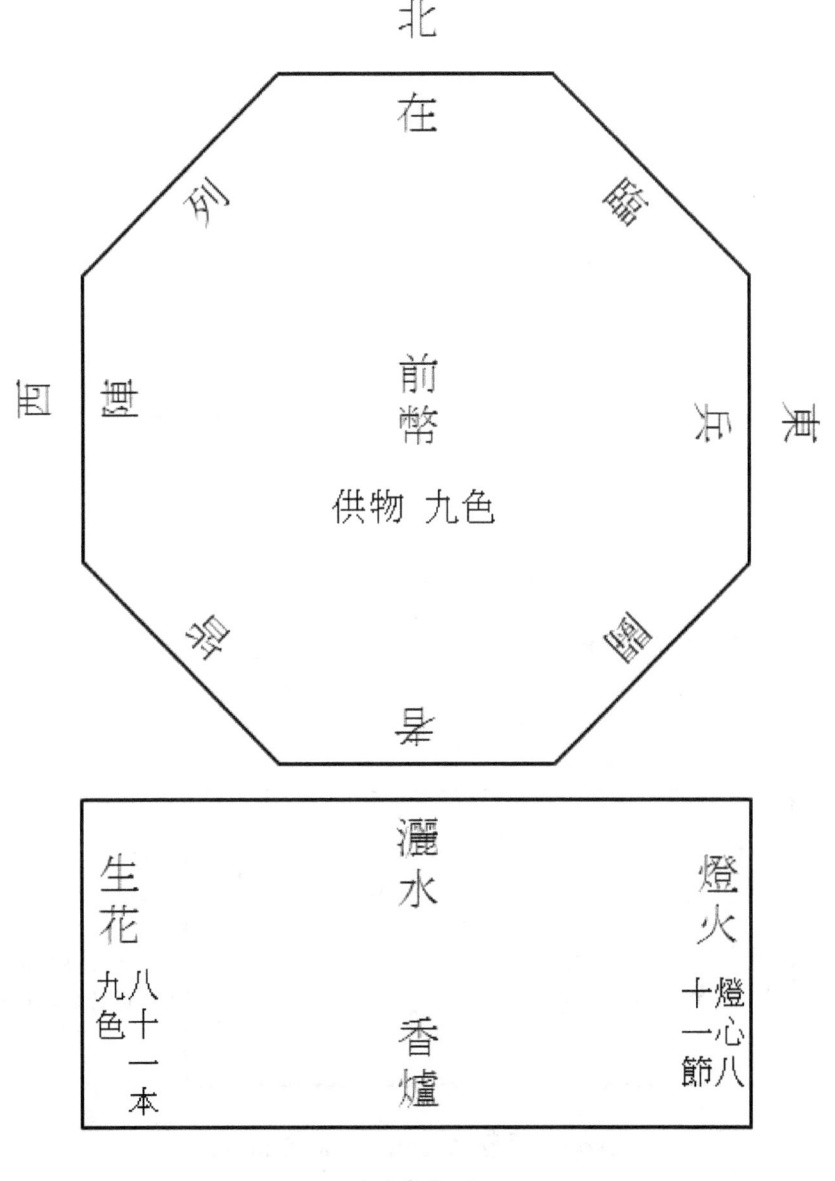

Transcription of Altar with Translation

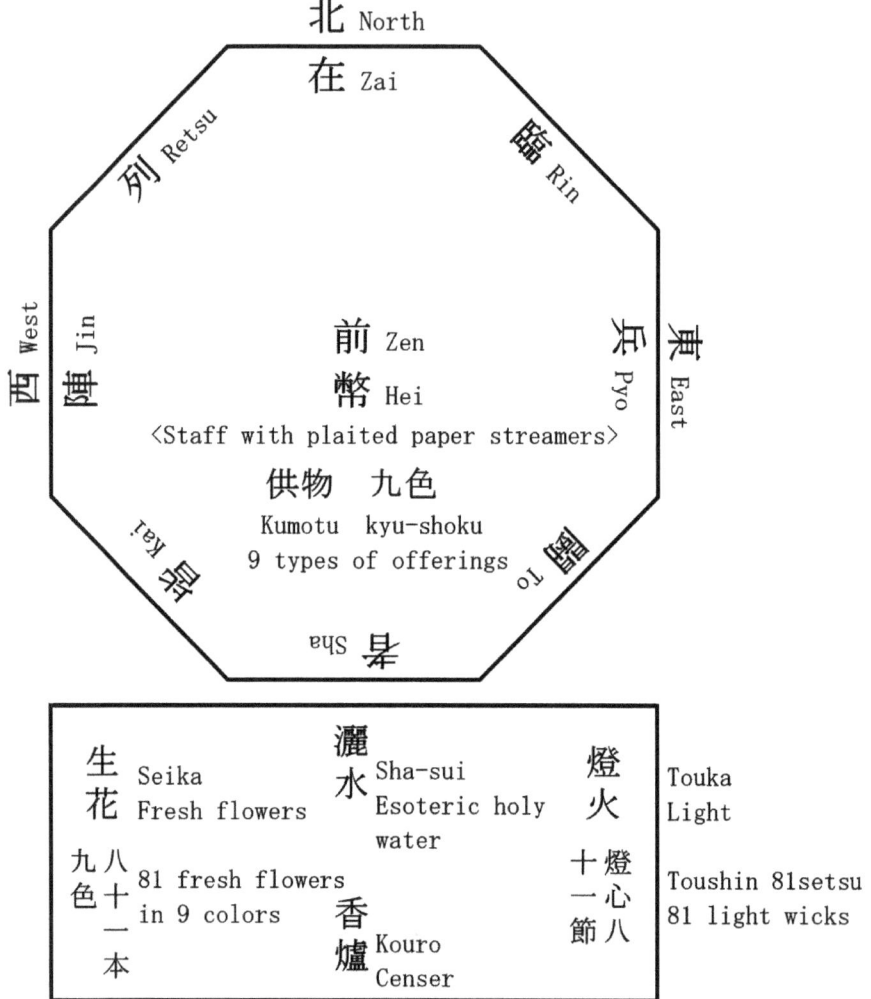

Dan Hoshiki 檀法式
How to Prepare the Altar

The bottom board of the altar should be an octagon with each side being 9 Sun and 9 Bun, 12 inches/30 centimeters long. There should be four octagon shaped legs with each leg being 9 Bun, 1 inch/2.7 centimeters, wide and 2 Shaku 7 Sun, 32 inches/81 centimeters tall. Paper banners should be placed on each side of the octagon. Make a protective ward by drawing the first eight Kanji of the Kuji, namely:

臨 兵 鬥 者 皆 陣 列 在
Rin, Pyo, Toh, Sha , Kai, Jin, Retsu, Zai
Face, Soldier, Fight, Person, Everything, Legion, Arrange, Exist

The *Hei* 幣 Shinto staff tied with folded paper streamers in the center serves as the final Kanji Zen 前.

The poles holding the paper streamers should be 9 Sun, 10.6 in/27 cm, the paper streamers should be 9 Sun vertical and 9 Sun horizontal.

七五三ノ外ニ幕ヲウツ也。行者浄衣
ヲ着ス。七日八十一座壇ニ入ナリ。齋
ハ云ニ不及ナリ

一 引目ヲ射ル三九度ナリ。鳴弦ヲモ
行ベシ。弦ヲキル九字ニ中ルナリ。引
ハ幕目ノ本字・

符守之法

前前前前前前前

両行長八寸一分宛
中長九寸
幅九分

右上ノ包〆九字ノ文字ヲ上ノ包ニ書ス

The rope makes a curtain around the altar. The *Gyosha*, or practitioner, should wear a robe that has been purified.[98] You should pray eighty-one times over the course of seven days. It goes without saying that the one doing the praying should obey all Buddhist admonitions and fast from the noonday meal until the following morning.

---

[98] The author does not specify the type of robe, however for Shinto ceremonies, a white robe made of cotton cloth or silk is worn.

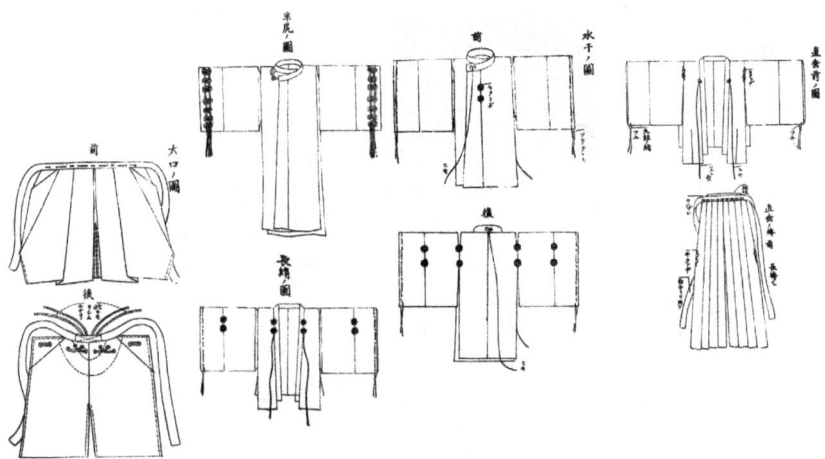

Shoot *Hikime*⁹⁹ arrows with a carved whistle as an arrowhead. These whistling arrows should be fired according to the San-San-Ku 三々九 a three, three, nine pattern shooting ceremony.¹⁰⁰

---

⁹⁹ *Hikime* 蟇目, whistling arrow. Hikime can be written with Kanji meaning Toad's Eye. This is thought to refer to how the openings that allow air in resemble a toad's eye, or that the mysterious whistling sound resembles a toad croaking. These arrows were fired over the houses of high ranking Samurai when a child was born in order to dispel evil. They were also used in various sport shooting competitions, no doubt to add drama to the event. The whisling arrowheads can be made of bone or wood and have 5 to 8 openings across the tip.
Illustration of Hikime arrows from *Illustrated Bow and Arrow* 弓矢之図 1853

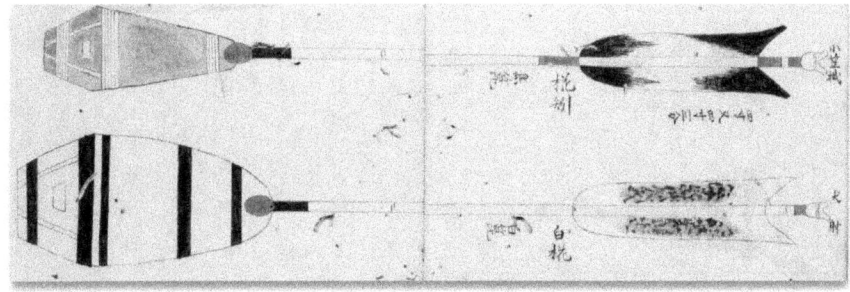

¹⁰⁰ In this ceremony a Hikime arrow is fired at a wooden board with cuts in it making nine quadrants, called *Igeta* 井桁 well-columns. Three rows of three making nine. It is mounted on a bamboo stake and the archer uses a Hikime arrow to shatter it.

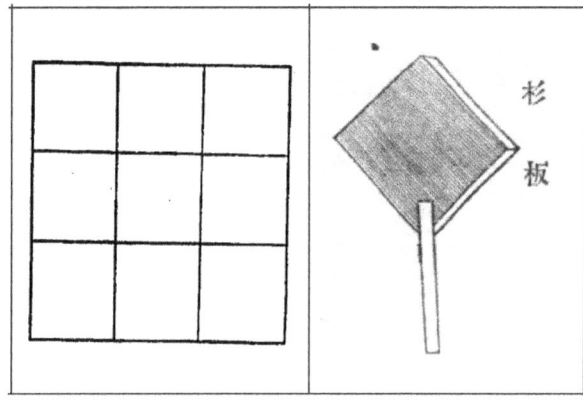

Meigen[101] plucking the bowstring without an arrow nocked, should also be done. Pluck the bowstring as if you are drawing the Kuji. When writing the word *Hikime* in Kanji, typically the combination 引目 pull + eye is used, however the original way it was written was 蟇目 toad + eye.

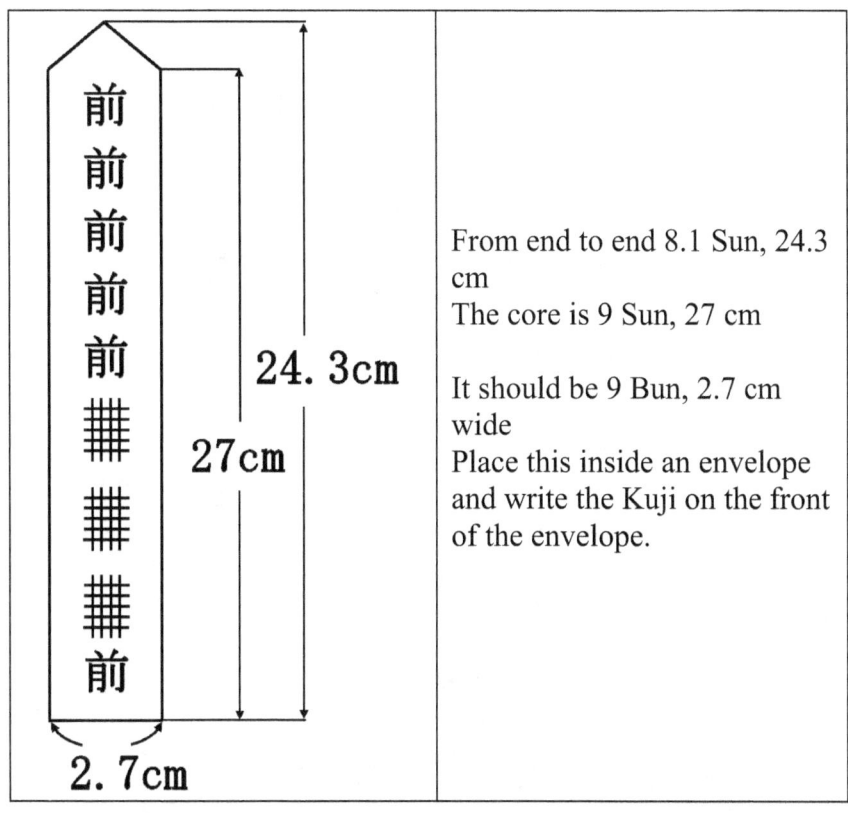

From end to end 8.1 Sun, 24.3 cm
The core is 9 Sun, 27 cm

It should be 9 Bun, 2.7 cm wide
Place this inside an envelope and write the Kuji on the front of the envelope.

Finally, you should write the Kuji on the front of the envelope.

Rin, Pyo, Toh, Sha , Kai, Jin, Retsu, Zai, Zen
臨　兵　闘　者　皆　陣　列　在　前
Face, Soldier, Fight, Person, Everything, Legion, Arrange, Exist, Before

---

[101] *Meigen* 鳴弦 "bird's call bowstring" is dry firing the Bo. This serves to banish any evil creatures or sprits that may be about. It was traditionally done before the emperor got in the bath, became ill or a son was born.

上書　臨兵闘者皆陣列在前

右折カケ包ナリ。灑水ニ辰砂龍骨虎ノ骨ヲ和メ書也。熊野牛王ノ黒燒ニ辰砂ヲ和メモ可ナリ。亦一寸香ヲ墨ニ和メモ用灑水生花共ニ井花水ヲ用ベシ。生花ハ草木交用灑水害花生ハ土ノ物ノ燒物ヲ用。供物ハ土器ニ盛也。亦墨ハ南天ノ黒燒ヲ用。香ハ沈香也。水ニハ水ノ習アリ流ニ依テ傳アリ。

一　水ニ九ノ水ノ秘傳ヲ記ス。大元ノ水造化。今是ニ一家ノ秘傳ヲ記ス。化ノ水。青龍ノ水。流行ノ水。化育ノ水。生成ノ水。金

The Kuji should be written with ink made from a mixture of powdered Dragon Sand (cinnabar,) Dragon Bone (fossilized mammals) and Tiger Bone mixed with *Shasui*, Purifying Water.[102] Another method is to use *Kuroyaki* 黒焼 Charred Medicine, from *Kumano Go-O* 熊野牛王 Cow-Headed King of Kumano Shrine, blended with Dragon Sand.[103] In addition it is also effective if you use *Issun Ko* purifying powdered incense mixed with ink.

Both *Shasui*, Purifying Water, and Ikebana, the art of flower arranging, use *Seikasui*, "flower well water" water drawn from a well between the hours of the Ox and the Tiger (2:00 ~ 4:00 a.m.)

---

[102] *Shasui* 灑水 (Kanji are purified + water) *Shasui* can also be written with the single Kanji 灑 or with the two-Kanji combination 洒水 (wash + water.) Both 灑 and 洒 mean to wash and purify. *Shasui* is used to cleanse the body, the Dojo, and other buildings or rooms. Purifying is done by dipping a wooden stick called a *Sanjo* 散杖 (Kanji are scattering + stick) or 灑水杖 (Kanji are *Shasui* + stick.) A bowl of perfumed water is prepared for performing *Shasui* purification. The stick is dipped in the water and used to sprinkle the water on your body or around a room. This serves to purify the body and mind and invokes the Buddha's nature. The idea is to sprinkle the water of the Buddha's wisdom and make the seeds of Bosatsu grow.

[103] *Kuroyaki* is medicine made from charred plants animals or insects. The charcoaled remains are mixed with various types of oil or water to create medicine. It is not clear what type of charcoal medicine was sold at the Kumano shrines.

Ikebana makes use of both plants and trees. The Shasui is poured into a container. Ikebana uses pottery that has been fired so that the container still feels rough. When making an offering an earthenware pot is filled. Further the ink should be made from Southern Heaven wood[104] that has been turned to charcoal. The ink is perfumed with *Jinko* 沈香, Agarwood.[105]

---

[104] 南天 Southern Heaven, a shrub commonly used in Japanese style gardens and as Bonsai. Produces a small red berry. Since the leaves turn red in fall, they are used in new year's decorations.

[105] Agarwood or the Wood of Gods, is a fragrant wood used in incense, perfume and small carvings. It is formed when the Aquilaria becomes infected with a type of Phaeoacremonium mold. The tree defensively secretes a resin to combat the fungal infestation. Prior to becoming infected, the heartwood is mostly lacking in scent, and is relatively light and pale in coloration. However, as the infection advances, and the tree produces its fragrant resin as a final option of defense, the heartwood becomes very dense, dark, and saturated with resin.

生ノ水、潤下ノ水、中和ノ水、以上九ノ水十リ

九水之式

臨造化水	在大元水	列潤下水
丘青龍水	前中和水	陣金生水
闢流行水	者化青水牢	皆生成水

太ノ元ノ水ハ灑水ヲ用ベシ。
化ノ水ハ海水ヲ用ベシ。
青龍水ハ瀧ノ水ヲ用ベシ。

北一流榊ノ
一枝置露ノ造
北似人ノ
一口溜水
一流木
二置

水也。

Kyusui 九水, the Nine Waters

There are many lessons about *Kyusui* 九水, the Nine Waters. The way these are prepared depends on the school. I will record one secret method that has been passed down. The Nine Waters are as follows:

1. *Junkasui* 潤下水 Moistening Descending Water
   Water flowing downward freely and unobstructed and not being colored by anything it passes.
2. *Taigensui* 太元水 Water of the Origin of All Things, the source of all things
3. *Zoukasui* 造化水 Water of Creation and Nurturing
   All things between heaven and earth are born, destroyed, and transformed. Existence is without limit.
4. *Kinjousui* 金生水 Water of Metal Attributes/ Producing Metal
   The unification of water and metal based on the Five Agents, Fire, Water, Wood, Metal, and Earth. Water is said to generate from freezing on the surface of metal. (It is one of the five elements of the Five Elements Theory.)
5. *Chuwasui* 中和水 Water of Harmony
   To be unbiased and correct in character, emotion, and nature. Being harmonious. To be moderately calm.
6. *Seiryusui* 青龍水 Water of the Azure Dragon
   The Azure Dragon is one of the divine creatures that guard each direction of the compass. The Kanji are blue + dragon however in this era the blue refers to a vibrant green. The Azure Dragon controls spring.
7. *Seiseisui* 生成水 Water of Generation
   Emergence of life and its growth and development
8. *Kaikusui* 化育水 Water of Creating and Nurturing
   That heaven, earth, and nature give birth to and nurture all things.
9. *Ryukousui* 流行水 Water of Flowing and Spreading
   The natural flow of water in a stream as it spreads out.

SECRETS OF THE KUJI・九字秘傳

***Kyusui no Shiki* 九水之式**
How the Nine Waters are Combined with the Kuji (Transcript)

北

列潤下水	在太元水	臨造化水
陣金生水	前中和水	兵青龍水
皆生成水	者化育水	闘流行水

西 東

南

Kyusui no Shiki 九水之式
How the Nine Waters are Combined with the Kuji
(Transcript with English Translation)

北 〈Kita〉:North

列 Retsu 潤下水 Junkasui: Water of Moistening and going down	在 Zai 太元水 Taigensui: Water of the origin of all things	臨 Rin 造化水 Zoukasui: Water of creation and nurturing
陣 Jin 金生水 Kinjousui: Water of Metal Attributes/ Producing metal	前 Zen 中和水 Chuwasui: Water of being in harmony	兵 Pyo 青龍水 Seiryusui: Water of the Azure Dragon
皆 Kai 生成水 Seiseisui: Water of generation	者 Sha 化育水 Kaikusui: Water of creating and nurturing	闘 To 流行水 Ryukousui: Water of flowing and spreading

西 〈Nishi〉:West 東 〈Higashi〉:East

南 〈Minami〉:South

Retsu –	Junkasui :	Moistening Descending Water
Zai –	Taigensui:	Water of the Origin of All Things
Rin –	Zoukasui:	Water of Creation and Nurturing
Jin –	Kinjousui:	Water of Metal Attributes/ Producing Metal
Zen –	Chuwasui:	Water of Harmony
Pyo –	Seiryusui:	Water of the Azure Dragon
Kai –	Seiseisui:	Water of Generation
Sha –	Kaikusui:	Water of Creating and Nurturing
Toh –	Ryukousui:	Water of Flowing and Spreading

一、

流行水ハ流水ヲ用ベシ。一ノ流レ結界ノ清メ
水ニ用ユ。露ハ天一ノ化育水ハ七度熱所ノ冷
水ヲ置露也。南天ノ露シテ田地ニ流レ花水ヲ用ヒ
葉水ニ用ベシ。生成ノ水ハ池水ヲ用ベシ。流水ヲ用ベシ。金生ノ水ハ泉水ヲ用ベシ。用ベシ。流ノ巣ニ流水ヲ置ニ露ヲ用。井花水ヲ用ベシ。山中和水ハ雨水ヲ用ベシ。煎ノ流レ清濁度此外説々ハ閣之。
物ノ類或ハ離魂又ハ傳死病萬ノ
託ノ法ニテ不治モノ無。
病邪崇ナド右ノ法ニテ
生靈死靈同更ナリ。其靈驗ハ行者ノ
德ニアリ。之ヲ三元護身之法ト云フ。
余ハ行者ノ心ニ有ベシ

How to Collect the Nine Waters

For *Taigensui* 太元水, Water of the Origin of All Things, *Shasui*, Purifying Water is used. However, some schools teach that dew should be collected from the branches growing on the north side of a Kashiwa evergreen tree.

Collect *Zoukasui* 造化水, Water of Creation and Nurturing, from Sea Trees.[106] Some schools teach that this water should be obtained from the water that collects in cut pieces of bamboo. They call this water *Sennin Sui*, Taoist Immortal Water.

For *Seiryusui* 青龍水, Water of the Azure Dragon, collect water from a waterfall. Some schools teach that this water should be collected from mist on the leaves of trees.

Collect *Ryukousui* 流行水, Water of Flowing and Spreading, from a source of flowing water, like a spring. Some schools teach that this water should be collected the water from an area that has had a purifying barrier around it or collect the mist from the Southern Heaven shrub.

Collect *Kaikusui* 化育水, Water of Creating and Nurturing, by boiling and cooling water seven times. Some schools teach that this water should be collected from Ikebana, referring to the mist that collects on the leaves or petals of a flower arrangement.

Collect Seiseisui 生成水, Water of Generation, from a pond. Some schools teach that you should use water from a field. This is referring to the water in a rice field.

---

[106] Details unknown. Probably refers to driftwood or beach vegetation washed up on the seashore.

Collect *Kinjousui* 金生水, Water of Metal Attributes/Producing Metal, from a spring. Some schools teach that this water should be collected from the mist that collects on potato leaves.

Collect *Junkasui* 潤下水, Moistening Descending Water, from rainwater. Some schools teach that this water should be collected from ponds on the top of a mountain.

Collect *Chuwasui* 中和水, Water of Harmony, from *Seikasui*, "flower well water" water drawn from a well between the hours of the Ox and the Tiger (2:00 ~ 4:00 a.m.) Some schools teach that this water should be collected from water that has been boiled seven times until it is clear. In other words, when boiling ingredients to make incense, skim off the clear water on top.

There are many other variations on the above methods of collecting water, however I will not include them here.

Tsukimono 憑物
Treating Demonic Possession

The previously mentioned spell is effective for people afflicted with *Tsukimono* 憑物, demonic possession, *Rikon* 離魂, when the soul has separated from the body, *Denshibyo* 伝死病 tuberculosis, *Mannobyo* 万の病 "any and all diseases" or *Jashu* 邪宗 a person captured by a religious cult[107] and so on. There is nothing it can't heal.

---

[107] In the Edo Era this could have referred to Christianity as well as other religions.

The *Reiken* 霊験 miraculous efficiency of this is well known to *Gyosha* 行者 acetic practitioners. This method is known as *Sangen Goshin no Ho*, the Three Parts of the Year Self-Defense Method.[108]

---

[108] The "Three Parts of the Year" are:
Jogen, Upper Third, namely the fifteenth day of January.
Chugen, Middle Third, namely the fifteenth day of the seventh month.
Gegen, Lower Third, the fifteenth day of the tenth month.

It can also refer to three cycles of the stems and branches, or 180 years. Thus, *Jogen*, Upper Third, refers to the first sixty years of this cycle, *Chugen*, Middle Third, refers to the second sixty years and *Gegen*, Lower Third, refers to the final sixty years. Referring to Ten-Chi-Jin, Heaven-Earth-Man. This also references *Tenhenchi-i* 天変地異 all phenomena that occur in the heavens or on the earth, including anything affecting man.

飯縄九字之事

凡飯縄ノ繩ハ伊律那之法ハ異國ニ於テモ
有之。虎ヲ本トスルニ異國ニ於テモ
法ト云。是吒吉尼天ノ法ナリ。白虎轉輪
イヅナ山ニ此天ノ宮アリ。故ニ我邦ノ
ノ名トス。此法精ク別ニ記シ置此法

肩八千肩三胸四腋五腰六足七足八腰九
男女

右九字ナリ。切法先擎吉尼ノ卯
ヲ強クシムルナリ。右手ヲ直ニ不動。
左手ヲ直ニ用テ四堅五横ニ
男女ニ依テ用圖ノ如クナリ。左右ニヨル切リ也。

Izuna Kuji no Koto 飯綱九字之事
Kuji Dedicated to Izuna[109]

Izuna Gongen[110]

    The Kuji of Izuna, written with the Kanji meal + rope or with three Kanji 伊律那 that sound out the name Izuna phonetically. This method is used all over Japan.

---

[109] Izuna, who has been worshiped since the 13th century is enshrined in a Shrine on the summit of Mt. Izuna in Nagano Prefecture. Izuna is often depicted as a Tengu, mountain goblin, riding a white fox.

[110] *From :An Illustrated Guide to Buddhist Deities* By Tosa Hidenobu 土佐秀信
Published 1900, illustrations based on book from 1690

Dakiniten

Since the spell is based on *Tora*, the tiger, it can also be referred to as *Hakko Tenrinho* 白虎転輪法, Revolving Wheel of the White Tiger Method. This is also referring to the *Dakiniten* 荼枳尼天[111] method.

There is a temple dedicated to Dainiten on Mt. Izuna.[112] That is why the name is the Nine Seals of Izuna. This method will be discussed in the following section.

---

[111] *Dakiniten* 荼枳尼天, also known as *Dakini* 荼枳尼 are Buddhist demonesses who eat the flesh and vital essence of humans.

The flesh eating demonesses are said to know when a person will die six months in advance. While they originate in Hindu texts, after being introduced in Japan, Dakini became associated with fox spirits and have therefore been incorporated into the Inari belief system.

[112] Izuna Mountain 飯縄山 is a 6,289 foot/1917 meter tall volcanic mountain located in northern Nagano Prefecture. Izuna Jinja shrine is at the top. This shrine is used by Shugendo practitioners for ascetic training. According to the author, this shrine is also a temple to Dakiniten.

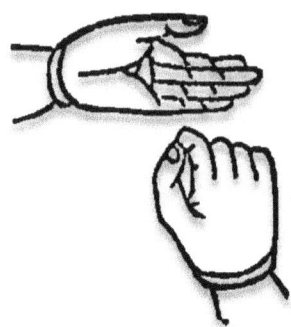

Mudra of the Flesh Eating Demonesses.

The way to perform the Kuji Dedicated to Izuna is to make the above mudra with your hands. This is the *Dakiniten no In* 荼枳尼天の印, the Mudra of the Flesh Eating Demonesses. The Kuji should be done as follows.

				Four Vertical
				Five Horizontal
Men	9	*Kata* 肩 Shoulder	1	Women
	8	*Te* 手 Hand	2	
	7	*Kata* 肩 Shoulder	3	
	6	*Mune* 胸 Chest	4	
	5	*Waki* 脇 Armpits	5	
	4	*Koshi* 腰 Hips	6	
	3	*Ashi* 足 Legs	7	
	2	*Ashi* 足 Legs	8	
	1	*Koshi* 腰 Hips	9	

When making the cuts your right hand should not move and your left should immediately draw the four vertical and five horizontal lines of the Kuji grid. The method differs for men and women. It should be done as shown in the illustrations. The five vertical and five horizontal lines should be drawn from right to left.

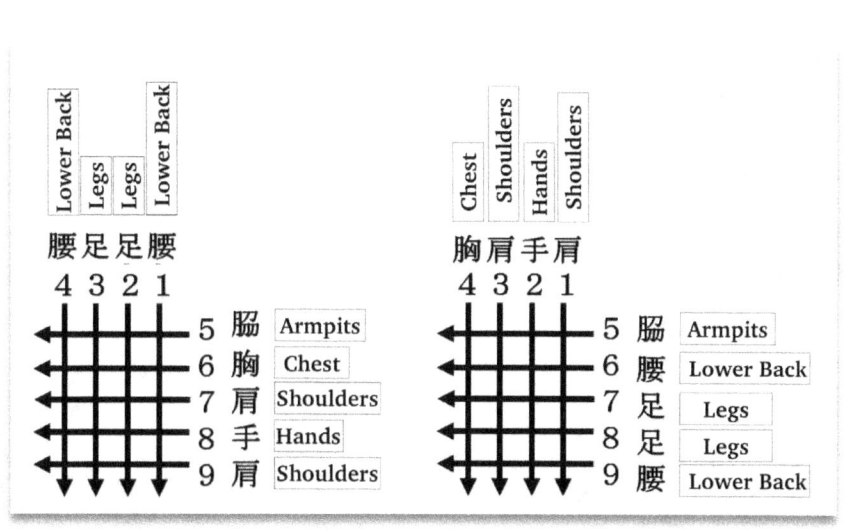

Men should chant the following as they cut the Kuji,

Koshi, Ashi, Ashi Koshi, Waki, Mune, Kata, Te, Kata
Hips,[113] leg, leg, hips, armpits, chest, shoulders, hands, shoulders

Women should chant the following as they cut the Kuji,

Kata, Te, Kata, Mune, Waki, Koshi, Ashi, Ashi, Koshi
Shoulders, hands, shoulders, chest, armpits, hips, leg, leg, hips

---

[113] The word *Koshi* 腰 or hips can refer to the lower back as well as the hips. Also *Ashi* 足 can refer to either the foot or leg.

解法ハ先ヅ卯ヲ解テ、右ノ手ヲ延テ、左ノ手ノ如ク二、四、竪五、横ニ切モドスナリ。左ヨリ。
右ヘ切。女ノ時ハ男ノ法ニ、男ノ時ハ
女ノ法ニ、九字ヲ誦スルナリ

柏手　唵𡀔吉尼耶娑婆訶　三遍

応弾　隅母　　　　　　　三遍

一　癰疾ノ厭勝譬ハ男五十歳十ヲバ、九
ヲ去テ余五、臍ニ字ヲ用。或ハ三十歳ハ、
九ヲ去テ余三、足ニ字ヲ用。女四十一歳ハ、
九ヲ去テ余四、胸ニ字ヲ用ルナリ。九ヲ

You must release the spell after you use it. The first step is undoing the Mudra. Undo the Mudra by extending your right hand. Then use your right hand to draw the four vertical and five horizontal lines the same way you used your left hand to draw the four vertical and five horizontal lines except that you are cutting from left to right.

Illustration showing how to release the Kuji Dedicated to Izuna.

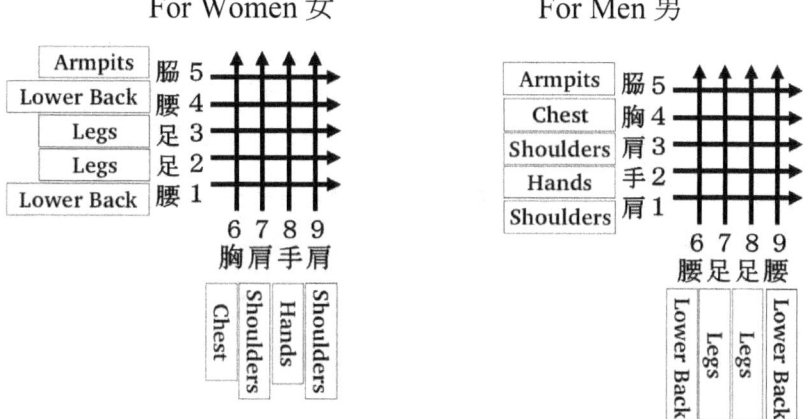

Further, when releasing this spell, women should do the Kuji for men and men should do the Kuji for women.

Men should chant the following as they cut the Kuji,

Kata, Te, Kata, Mune, Waki, Koshi, Ashi, Ashi, Koshi
Shoulders, hands, shoulders, chest, armpits, hips, leg, leg, hips

Women should chant the following as they cut the Kuji,

Koshi, Ashi, Ashi Koshi, Waki, Mune, Kata, Te, Kata
Hips, leg, leg, hips, armpits, chest, shoulders, hands, shoulders

Finally, clap while chanting *On-Da-Kini-Ya-Sowaka* three times and snap your fingers while chanting *Gubo* 隅母[114] three times.

---

[114] Unknown meaning.

去ノ法ハ、九ニ満ルヽ数ヲ去ルヽナリ。九
ヨリ内ハ直ニ用ルヽ也。右ノ年中リ用
字ヲ男ハ左女ハ右各其脇ツボニ筆
スベシ。字ノ上ヲ塗ニ墨ヲ以ス。他見ヲ
不レ許ナリ。發日ノ朝用ヲ可トス。赤其
日ニ非メモ可ナリ
一齒ノ痛ニ。右ノ如ク男女ノ。歳中リノ
用ノ字ヲ其人ノ口ヲ開サセテ。小刀ヲ
以テ其痛ム所ヲ志メ畫スベシ

九字解之支
凡九字ハ、太陽ノ結果ニメ、繋縛ノ理

Gyakushitsu[115] Imminent Fevers, can be suppressed through spells. For example, if a man is fifty years old, he should subtract nine from his age, until he ends up with a number equal to or less than nine. In this case the answer would be five. Then chant

Koshi, Ashi, Ashi Koshi, Waki, Mune, Kata, Te, Kata
Hips, leg, leg, hips, armpits, chest, shoulders, hands, shoulders

Since the fifth Kanji is Waki, armpits, that is the one he should use.

Another example is a man who is thirty years old. That person should subtract nine from thirty until they end up with a number equal to or less than nine, in this case the person would end up with three. The third Kanji in the sequence is Leg, so that is the one he would use.

A forty year old woman would start to subtract nine from her age until she ends up with four. The sequence used by women is chant,

Kata, Te, Kata, Mune, Waki, Koshi, Ashi, Ashi, Koshi
Shoulders, hands, shoulders, chest, armpits, hips, leg, leg, hips

Since the fourth Kanji is Mune, chest, would use that Kanji.

This method of removing a series of nines serves to remove all nines. Immediately, use whichever Kanji ends up as a result of the subtraction. You should draw the Kanji that results based on your age in the depression in the armpit. Men should draw it under their left armpit, women under their right. Finally, paint over the Kanji with ink. This is to prevent anyone else from seeing it. It should be applied on the morning of the onset of fever. It must only be done on that day.

Treating Toothaches

For tooth pain, determine the appropriate Kanji from the Kuji based on the man or woman's age. Then take a Shoto, short sword, and have the patient open their mouth. Determine the location of the pain and, while focusing write the appropriate Kanji on that spot.

---

[115] Gyakushitsu 瘧疾 intermittent fever; the shakes; malarial fever

ナリ。故ニ歊ヲ縛テ不動ナリ。是ヲ以
解カズンバ有ベカラズ拍子ヲウチ
彈指ヲナスレバ解ルナリ呪ニ曰、唵縛
日ー羅納舎克。之ヲ誦テ三度拍キスレ
バスベテ壓縮ヲ解ルナリ。術者馬顔
香ヲ以テ解鎖戸透ヲナスニ。此呪ヲ
用ユト云ヘリ。無用ノ事ナレバ精ク
セス。松脂ヲ火ニ燒バ馬顔香ハ消ル
ナリ。邪術ヲ破ルニ。九字ヲ行ヘバ速
ニ破ルナリ。急用秘傳九字ヲ仰テ。
實瓶卯ニテ陰形ヲ修シテ。四竪五横
ニ切ルベシ。忽ニ邪術ハ破ルナリ。旦

Kuji Kai no Koto 九字解之叓
Releasing the Kuji Dedicated to Izuna

The underlying principle of Kuji spells is to create a boundary ward based on Taiyo, the Sun. It is important to note that once you have applied to your enemy, he will be bound and unable to move. For that reason you must release the spell. To release the spell, clap your hands and snap your fingers.

Chant the divine phrase *On-Ba-Sarado-Tokoku* and clap three times to release the spell you cast. This will loosen the bonds of the spell.

The practitioner should chant the spell *On-Ba-Sarado-Tokoku* while using Seeing a Horse Face in Incense Smoke [116] in order to employ the spell Kaisato Suki, Unlocking the Gate and Passing Through the Chain. This will allow you to see what your opponent fears.

---

[116] *Uma Gao Koh* 馬顔香 "Seeing a Horse Face in Incense Smoke" also referred to as *Jinmen Bamen* 人面馬面 Human Face, Horse Face. In the Edo period (1600~1868,) a book on *Tejina*, magic tricks, describes such a trick.

When a person holds their face in front of a fire, it is said their face will look like a horse's face, which is thought to be magical.

-Tejina
Edo Era

Take wolf dung and earthworms that have been dried in the shade and set them on fire. Have a person stand behind the smoke, and look at their face. This mysterious technique will make their face appear elongated. face of the person behind the smoke is seen for a long time. -The trick is to make beans on the horse's back, grind the beans into a powder, and then use the powder to make the horse's face appear long and shiny by pouring oil on it.

Another method is to crush the weathered skull of a horse and roll the powder into small tablets. When you are ready to use them, crush the tablet into powder. Take a piece of Koyori paper string and rub the powder into it. Finally, dip it in oil and light it on fire.

-Unravelling the Shinobi Scroll 忍之巻を読み解く
Ninjutsu Research Volume Two 忍術研究・2号 August 2019

As this method is unrelated, I will not go into details. If you burn pine sap, the Seeing a Horse Face in Incense Smoke will disappear.

If you employ Kuji to obliterate Jajutsu, an evil technique, understand it will be instantly effective. Emergency Secret Nine Seals using the *Ichi In Ju* 一印十, One Seal in Ten.[117] First make the Sacred Bottle mudra thereby activating Ingata, Yin Form, the opposite of the Sun, which is Yang. Then cut the four vertical and five horizontal lines. This will immediately effective against Jajutsu, evil spells, shattering their power. [118]

No matter what level of practitioner you are, beginner, intermediate or advanced, you must always release the spell in the end.[119] If you fail to do so, evil will blanket you and you will suffer. However, it should never be used carelessly except to save someone's life, or when you are in danger from an enemy. And do not neglect your training, something you should do from the hour of the tiger (3~5 am) to the hour of the cock (5~7pm,) two sixes a day.[120]

---

[117] The author writes One Seal as Ten. It is not clear if this means "A single seal represents ten true words." Another way of looking at it is "add another Kanji to the Kuji so you end up with ten."

[118] It is important to understand that by using the Kuji Dedicated to Izuna you are making a contract with the Dakiniten (Dakini,) Flesh Eating Demonesses. Thus it should only be used by a person with a deep faith in Dakini. Only a practitioner of that faith can safely use the Kuji Dedicated to Izuna without fear of retribution. It is also said that if the practice is not done correctly, not only will it be ineffective, but it may also offend Dakini. Dakini, in particular, is said to have been originally a demon god of the nightshade type who ate human flesh, and if one has faith in him and prays to him with the secret method, one can obtain outstanding spiritual blessings.

[119] *Shochugo* 初中後 The three stages of a thing: beginning, middle, and end. Often used in documents of this era to describe the stages of learning from novice to experienced.

[120] *Nirokuji Chu* 二六時中 A day was divided into twelve two-hour periods. "Two Sixes" is twelve. Another way to say all day.

初中後卯ヲ解クトナカレ。若懈ル時ハ反テ邪法ノ害ヲ蒙ルベシ。但シ身ニ敵友テ邪法ノ害ヲ蒙ルベシ。但シ身ニ敵スルカ、亦ハ人ヲ救フノ外ニ、全ク慎テナスコトモルベシ。亦修行ハ懈ルベカラズ。寅ニ酉ニ二六時中修行スベシ

解後誦文
刀兵不能害。水火不犯漂。得昇百歳。得見百秋安穏冨貴自在婆婆訶

右一心ニ誦スベキナリ三遍

右ハ兵家着流ノ傳來ナリ。大ニ暑キ如レ此ヲ是外品多トト雖。紙面長大ヲ恐テ止矣

九字秘傳終

Kaigo Zumon 解後誦文
A Spell to Chant After Releasing Kuji

Chant the following spell three times with all your spirit.

To-hyo funogai 刀兵不能害
The sword of the soldier does not harm you.
Suika, Fuhanhyo 水火不犯漂
Throughout your life you will neither be burned by fire nor will you be swept away by water.
Tokusho Hyakusai 得昇百歳
You will live to reach the age of a hundred.
Tokuken Hyakushu 得見百秋
You will see autumn a hundred times.
An-non Fuki Jizai 安穏冨貴自在
You will have wealth and power to wield freely.
Sowaka 娑婆訶 I pray[121]

The above is a method transmitted among *Heihoja*, warriors.[122] There are many other methods and forms, but this is generally how the methods are done. Adding all the possible variations will make this book too long, so I will stop here.

Kuji Hiden Owari 九字秘伝終
End of Secret Kuji Teachings

---

[121] Sowaka 娑婆訶 is a secret word used at the end of a mantra or darani to pray for the fulfillment of a wish. Originally, it meant a good offering.

[122] According to the *Tensei Hon Setsuyoshu* 天正本節用集, a dictionary written in 1590 a Heihoja 兵法者 is a person who excels at Kenjutsu and other martial arts. A soldier or military strategist.

無法復有法謂之術也無術復有妙也無妙復有妙謂之德也無德復有靈也無靈復有靈謂之神也故神者先于天地臭于萬物無不有神矣充塞六合無烏有烏者夫只神乎豈謂不至大哉昭二天理填二雷聲輕二雲烟鎧二白雲神乎否乎否乎無為神乎蓋神乎云神而神者也一滴一凍也無為有為者牙上生牙也有烏有烏有烏者也彼謂否者可謂有為有為者也彼謂無為是謂有為者可謂否否者也無風起波無事生事何謂獨步九天哉出没夭虛中吹毛曾不動何謂至

While there is no universal theory there is a method that can be done. This method is called Jutsu, meaning art or technique. While there is no universal art, there is an art that can be done. This art is called Myo, a mysterious and highly refined method. While there is no universal mysterious and highly refined method, there is a mysterious and highly refined method, a mysterious and highly refined method that can be done. What I am describing is Toku, or virtue. While there is no universal virtue, there is a virtue that can be held. This virtue is Rei, the divine spirit within you capable of employing supernatural power. While there is no universal Rei, there is a method of employing that power. This is referring to Kami, god, or the divine power that brings both misfortune and blessings to the world. Divine beings bestow blessings and mete out punishment on man. A Kami is a being that the ancients believed inhabited and controlled all things in heaven and earth. There is nothing that is not infused with the divine nature of Kami.

The fact is the Six Realms, heaven, earth and the four cardinal directions, all things, are completely full of both Mui and Ui.

Mui, means relying on nature. Nature is unchanging, the state of being unborn and immortal, apart from cause and effect.

Ui, is a way of being born and destroyed through cause and effect, so changing over time.

Since both Mui and Ui are infused with Kami, divinity, why then do people not feel this is the ultimate? The shining light of rule of heaven and the laws of nature and humanity. It speaks with a voice loud as thunder, but can be as light as clouds or smoke. When turned white, it is the whiteness of snow.

Is this Kami or denial of Kami? (Is this divinity or the denial of divinity?) Is this a denial of Kami or proof of Kami? (Is this a denial of divinity or proof of divinity?) Certainly this is Kami, divinity. Thus it can be said to be both Kami and a thing that will become Kami.

There is a saying that goes *One drop of Water, Falls to the Ground and Freezes.* This is referring to how water drips from an icicle and freezes a moment later. Our lifespans are like that falling drop of water and we should cherish each moment of our lives and the life we have been entrusted with to the fullest.

However, discussing Mui, means relying on unchanging nature, and Ui, constant change through being born and destroyed through cause and effect is kind of like a creature having one set of fangs grow down over its other fangs so it can no longer close its mouth.

Saying it is *Ui* 有為, cause and effect, means that it is Ui, cause and effect. This is another way of saying it is Kami, or divine. Understand that a man who says he follows Ui, should be considered to have said the opposite. Ui is Ui.

A man that says he follows *Mui* 無為, relying on nature, should be interpreted as meaning he follows Ui, cause and effect. This is because a negation is a negation.

If there is no wind, there will not be any waves in the ocean. So what needs to be said to bring forth action? Can one walk alone across *Kyuten*, all nine heavens, north, northeast, east, southeast, south, southwest, west, northwest and center?

Is it possible to enter and leave the great void of the universe freely and uninhibited, without your true nature being disturbed? To remain on the plateau of no-self, utterly free of polluting thoughts and worldly desires? The void of the universe is the sublime realm of acting without mind and without human intent. Like the famous sword *Wind Blowing a Single Hair*, which is so razor sharp it can slice in half a single hair floating in the breeze, you are both immovable and able to respond to the slightest change.

Nine-Nine-Eighty-One,[123] the whole universe, has neither east nor west.

---

[123] In ancient China the Earth was considered to be a square, while heaven a circle. Together they form the whole of the universe.
Half of the numbers 1~10 were assigned to the earth and half to heaven. According to the yin-yang five-element, the yang numbers are (1, 3, 5, 7, and 9) and the yin numbers are (2, 4, 6, 8, and 10)
The odd numbers fall and condense on the earth while the even numbers float to the heavens.
According to this theory, the circumference of a circle is represented by the number one, while its diameter is represented by three. This means the total of the heavens is four. As for the earth, it also has a diameter of one, and each side has a length of one. This means the total for earth is five. Adding four and five results in nine. Nine multiplied by nine is eighty-one. Thus Nine-Nine-Eighty-One represents heaven, earth, and nature.

大哉九九八十一本來無東西北行一回
亦為南先干天地盈干天地所謂神而神
者也昔者太公之助周道也是八十一為九九
而九者也始一終十十只歸于一
之夫太公所傳之九字矣天下之至道謂
至神道可謂獨步九天聖以神道一陰一陽一道謂治
一亂謂之三才變也古周公之所能化其
變所謂太公之所授而紫亂朱衰哉慎也後
世道衰邪說誣人以

天明丁未二月 南畝 宮安泰

If you are heading north and rotate, south will appear before you. Before *Tenchi*, Heaven and Earth, existed, there was Kami, a god that possessed all the divinity of Heaven and Earth, which filled the whole universe. That is how the Kami of Heaven and Earth came to be.

Long ago, the military strategist Duke Tai of Qi[124] assisted King Wen of Zhou to overthrow King Zhou of Shang [125].

This is an example of a person who used eighty-one by taking nine, and then taking another nine. The beginning is one, the end is ten, but understand that ten is only the return to one. Thus nine should be considered the ultimate.

The Kuji as taught by Duke Tai of Qi are an ultimate truth in the universe. It is Shinto, the way of the gods. Another way to refer to this would be *Kyuten ni Doppo*, Walking Alone Across the Nine Heavens.[126] It is also known as *Ichi-In-Ichi-Yo-Ichi-Chi-Ichi-Ran*, or One Yin, One Yang, One Unifying, One Sowing Chaos.[127]

---

[124] Duke Tai of Qi 太公望 (1128~1015 BC.) Also known as Jiang Ziya.

[125] The last ruler of the Shang dynasty, King Zhou of Shang, was a tyrant who spent his days with his concubines and randomly executing or punishing both peasants and high-high level officials. Jiang Ziya is said to have defeated Shang's supernatural protectors Qianliyan and Shunfeng'er by employing his powers as a Taoist immortal.

[126] 九天に独歩

[127] 一陰一陽一治一乱

In other words by employing Kuji you are causing changes to occur in the Sansai 三才, the Three Talents, referring to Ten-Chi-Jin, Heaven-Earth-Man. [128]

The ancient sages taught moral lessons regarding places where Shinto, the way of the gods, was used to affect changes in reality. This is the instruction that the Duke of Zhou received from Duke Tai of Qi. Following the defeat of the Shang Dynasty, the Kings of the Zhou Dynasty (1046 BC ~256 BC) continued to treasure the lessons of the Kuji and handle them with care.

---

[128] In ancient China developed a system whereby the universe could be divided into heaven, earth, and man. It is also called the three materials 三材. In the I Ching, the way of Heaven is represented by In-Yo 陰陽, Yin and Yang, the way of Earth is represented by Ju-Go 柔剛, Softness and flexibility overcomes strength and rigidity, the way of man is of Jin-Gi 仁義 benevolence and righteousness. Here, the human virtues of benevolence and righteousness are considered to conform to the natural laws of yin-yang and rigidity. In other words, man is not in conflict with nature, but seeks harmony with nature in the human world.

Unfortunately this practice declined in later generations and the lessons became distorted. There were even those that tried to repurpose Kuji for their own mischievous ends. It is like purple has been shoved in as vermillion withers away.[129]

Miyai Yasutai 宮井安泰
Published Tenmei 7 (1787)

---

[129] This refers to a line from the *Analects* by Confucius.
「惡紫之奪朱也，惡鄭聲之亂雅樂也，惡利口之覆邦家者」
Confucius said:
"*I loathe purple for replacing vermilion; I loathe the melodies of Zheng for corrupting classical music; I loathe the clever of tongue for undermining states and families.*"
Vermillion was traditionally regarded as the correct color for mourning garments in Zhou dynasty China. However, it was replaced by purple because fabrics made in that color were easier and cheaper to produce and considered to be more fashionable. Purple is an intermediary color while vermilion is a primary one. To Confucius, the adoption of it violated the purity of the ritual ceremonies.
                    -*Leadership Lessons from Confucius: A Slippery Slope*
                                                             Richard Brown

Recreations

Kuji as Transmitted by Duke Tai of Qi

Early in the morning, face the east where you can see the first rays of sunrise. If you are in the mountains face the ridgeline to the east, if you are in flatlands, face the horizon. Place the palm of your left hand on your chest and grip, while extending the five fingers of your right hand in front of you with your palm down.

Turn your hands palms down curl your fingers once toward you as if you are beckoning someone. Chant the incantation,

Rin 臨 (to) Face
The retainers are lined up like the Kanji mouth repeated three times.

Next, place your right palm above your heart and extend the fingers of your left hand out in front of you before lowering your hand. Chant the incantation,

Hei 兵 Soldier
Underneath sixteen coins, place the numbers one and an eight.

Next, turn the palms of your hands outward and hold them at the level of your chest. Chant the incantation,

Toh 闘 Fight
Plant a bean behind the gate and it will sprout one out of the earth.

Next, move the palms of your hands out to the left and right so they are on either side of your chest. Chant the incantation,

Sha 者 Person
When you write the twentieth, you are writing "two tens" and day.

Squeeze both palms in fists, press them both to your breast. Chant the incantation,

Kai 皆 Everything
Standing two abreast, the gold crows fly off

Extend the fingers of both hand and turn them towards yourself, placing them on your shoulders. Chant the incantation,

Jin 陣 Legion
There is a small monkey there alone pulling a cart. The monkey seems like he is part of a village.

Turn your palms so they are facing you and press them into your hips. Chant the incantation,

Retsu 列 Line
Remove the element meaning to damage from the right side of the Kanji to remain.

Extend both palms and press them into your knees. Chant the incantation,

Zai 在 Exist
The first person who holds power and authority holds the earth in front of him.

Raise both palms to form *Dozu* 斗衝, the north star. Chant the incantation,

Zen 前 Face
In the middle of the ninth month, polish one Katana.

Kuji for creating an Iron-Strong Self-Defense Ward

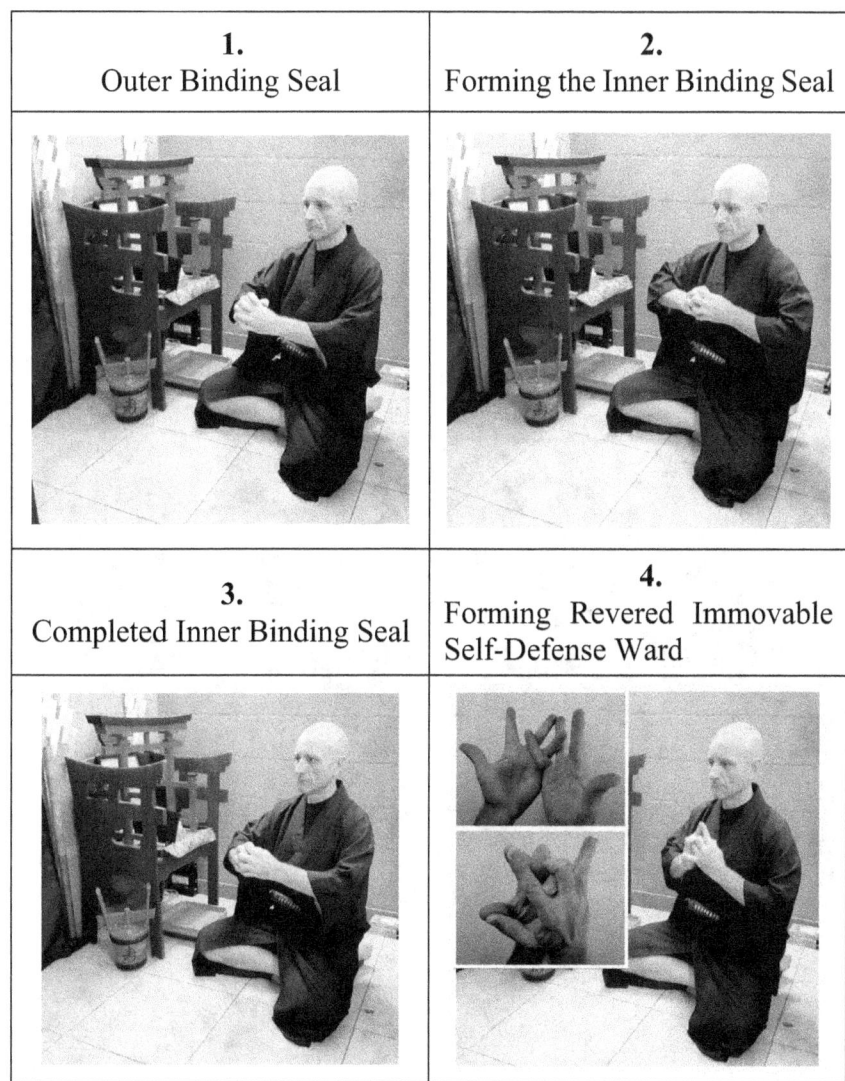

Chant the Kuji,
   Face, Soldier, Fight, Person, Everything, Legion, Arrange, Exist, Before

Completed Revered Immovable Self-Defense Ward

After chanting the Kuji with the above Mudra, next use your right hand to make the *Ken-in* 劔印 sword seal.

Bring your hands to your left hip, indicating sword in a scabbard.

Draw your sword and draw the four horizontal and five vertical lines.

How to Use the Kuji Dedicated to Marishiten

Form Outer Lion Seal and chant the Kuji, adding the Kanji *Sho* 勝 victory, to the end.

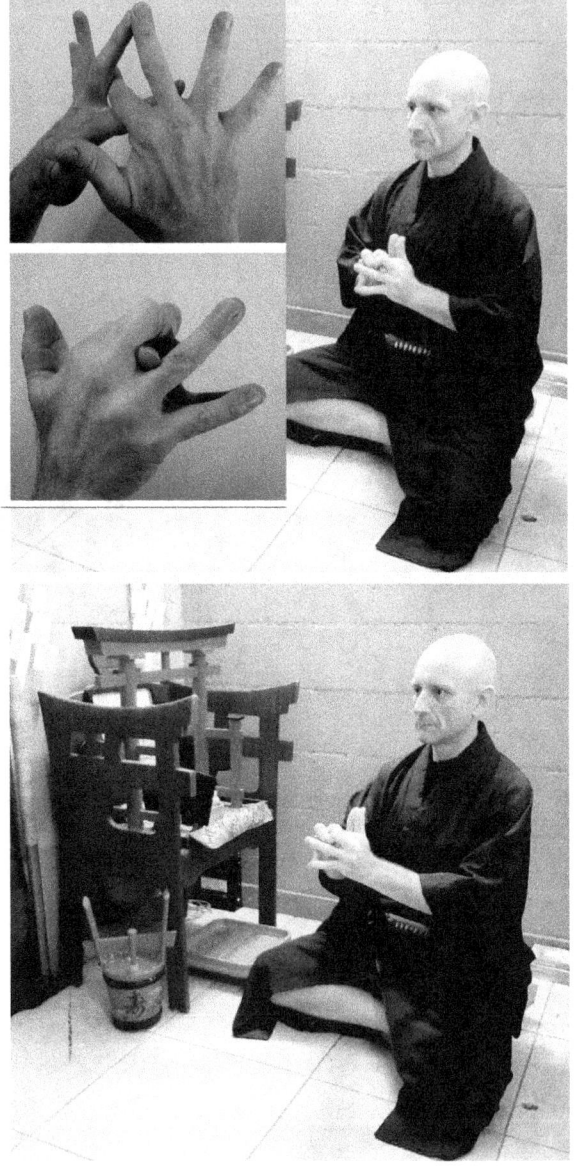

Face, Soldier, Fight, Person, Everything, Legion, Arrange, Exist, Before, Victory

Next form the Inner Lion Seal and chant the following,

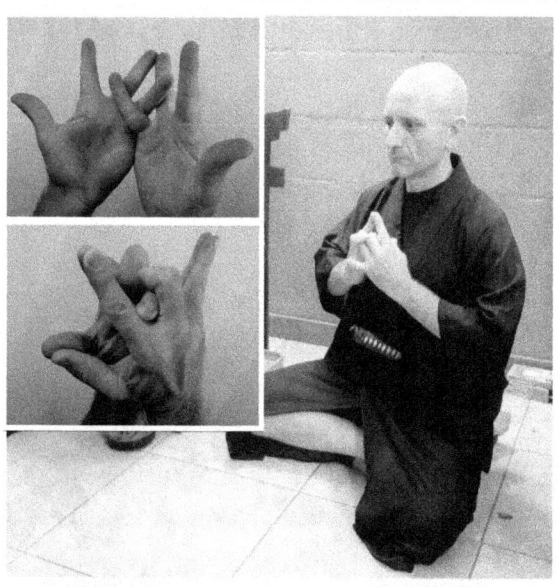

Chant: *On Marishi Ei Sowaka*
Meaning: *I will call your name anywhere and everywhere, please grant me your protection.*

Then form the Seal of the Horse Headed Wisdom King. Chant the following incantation. In this incantation the Kanji Zen is placed before Zai and the entire Kuji sentence takes on a slightly different meaning.

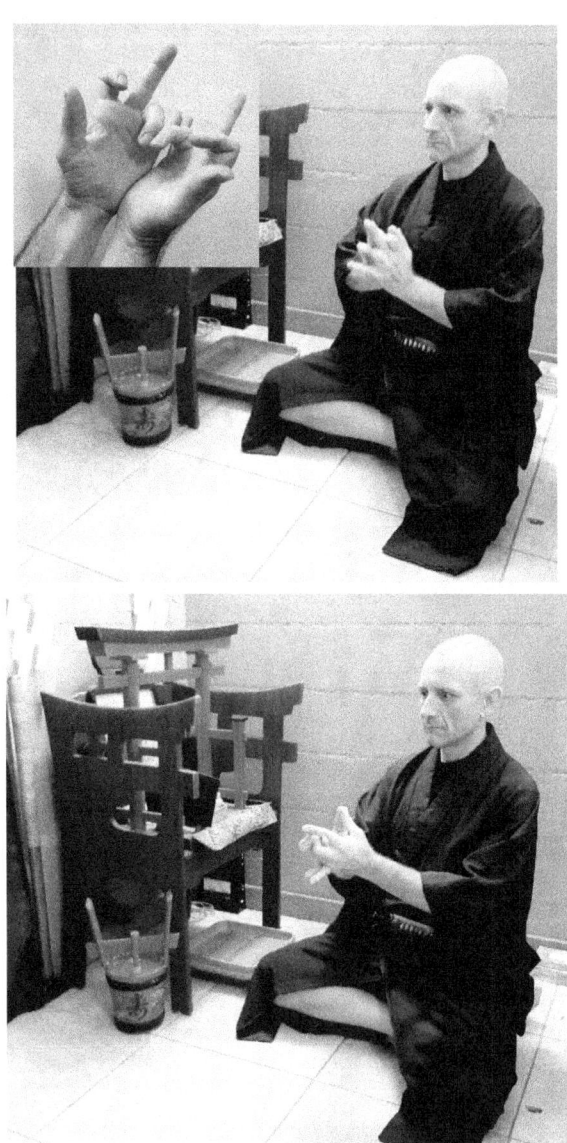

When facing a powerful Tsuwamono, soldier, those that seek to fight, all break out from the ranks and move to the vanguard.

Next, chant the following three times while making Ring of the Sun Seal.

Chant: *Nanmu Nichirin Marishiten Sowaka*
Meaning: *Praise Nichirin, the Sun, and Marishiten, the rays of light, please grant me your protection.*

Finally, form the Secret Shape Binding seal and chant the following three times. Then cut the Four Vertical and Five Horizontal Lines.

Chant: On Sen Da Ra Na Soku Sai Annon Meaning:...*Protect me from evil and disaster.*

After chanting the Kuji with the above Mudra, next use your right hand to make the *Ken-in* 劍印 sword seal.

Bring your hands to your left hip, indicating sword in a scabbard.

Draw your sword and draw the four horizontal and five vertical lines.

Gabriel Rossa is a woodworker who lives in Hawai'i and studies historical Ninjutsu, esoteric Buddhism and related subjects. He has contributed photos and information for numerous books including:

- *Samurai and Ninja* by Antony Cummins (2015)
- *The Lost Samurai School: Secrets of Mubyoshi Ryu* by Antony Cummins and Mieko Koizumi (2016)
- *The Dark Side of Japan* by Antony Cummins (2017)
- *Kuji* by Eric Shahan (2021)
- *Kuji* for Self Defense by Eric Shahan (2023).

www.ingramcontent.com/pod-product-compliance
Lightning Source LLC
Chambersburg PA
CBHW050440240426
43661CB00055B/2453